Discovering
New Brunswick

MARIANNE and H.A. EISELT

FORMAC PUBLISHING COMPANY LIMITED

HALIFAX

2002

Formac Publishing Company Limited acknowledges the support of the Cultural Affairs Section, Nova Scotia Department of Tourism and Culture. We acknowledge the financial support of the Government of Canada through the Book Publishing Industry Development Program (BPIDP) for our publishing activities. We acknowledge the support of the Canada Council for the Arts for our publishing program.

National Library of Canada Cataloguing in Publication Data

Eiselt, Marianne
        Discovering New Brunswick

Includes index.
ISBN 0-88780-556-6

        1. New Brunswick—Guidebooks. I. Title

FC2457.E56 2002   917.15'1044   C2002-901081-0
F1042.E56 2002

Formac Publishing Company Limited
5502 Atlantic Street
Halifax, Nova Scotia
B3H 1G4
www.formac.ca

Printed and bound in Canada.

Contents

Scenic Routes of New Brunswick

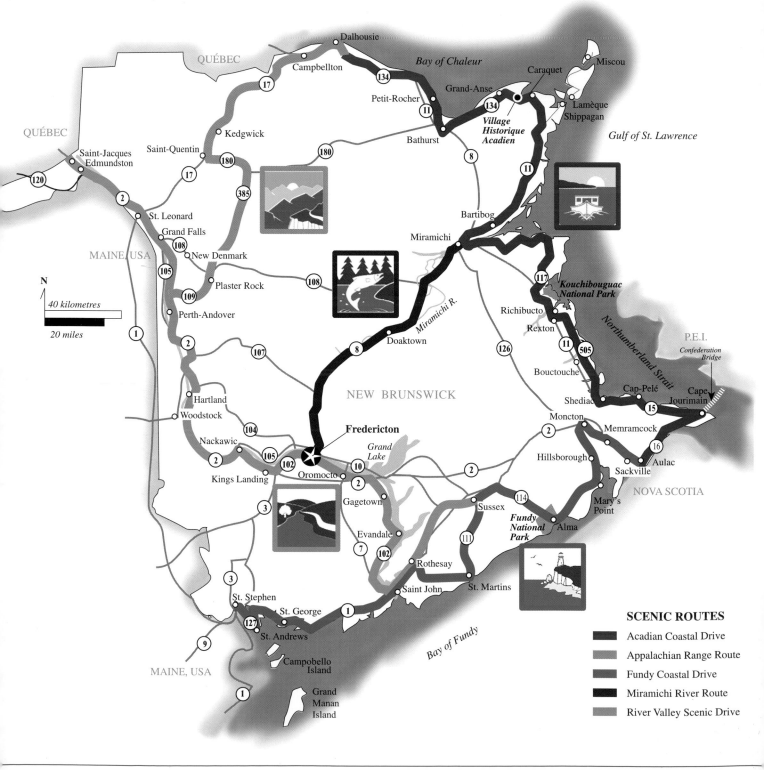

SCENIC ROUTES

- Acadian Coastal Drive
- Appalachian Range Route
- Fundy Coastal Drive
- Miramichi River Route
- River Valley Scenic Drive

Introduction

Fifteen years ago, when we made New Brunswick our home, my husband and I set out to discover what we could about the province. Driven by an urge to explore, we hiked along rugged, windswept coasts and dense hardwood ridges, we walked past huge glacial boulders and strolled along sandbars. We stood on top of the highest peak in the Maritimes. We slept in the wilderness, where black bears, moose and deer roam. Squirrels dashed over our tent at night. We got lost on the Dobson Trail, huddled fearfully together during thunder and lightning atop Mount Sagamook and high on Grand Manan's lonely cliffs. On our nature walks, we learned about the ways the Mi'kmaq and Maliseet used birch for canoes and sphagnum moss for diapers. We walked upon dykes, skillfully built by the Acadians to reclaim land for farming. The connection between the land and its inhabitants became clear. The more we hiked and later canoed, the more we wanted to know about the people.

This is how the idea of a cultural journey into the province was conceived and we set out to discover the human story behind the landscape. We found ourselves in a 3,000-year-old Indian village, now Red Bank First Nation. We looked over the island where the first French explorers Samuel de Champlain and Pierre Gua de Monts barely survived their first winter in 1604. We learned about the Acadians, their fate, tenacity and *joie de vivre*. We heard about their co-operation with the Indians and German settlers around Moncton. We learned about the 15,000 exiled Loyalists who fled the United States in 1783 and 1784, to settle on land they had been granted along the St. John River. We became aware of the many Irish, Scottish and English settlers who came to New Brunswick in hope of a better future. We listened to the stories of the Danes, whose descendants homesteaded in New Denmark and we heard about the Jewish families who worked and lived in Saint John. All these people left their mark on the province.

A cultural journey through the province's heritage and natural history museums, galleries and craft shops, convents and churches, courthouses and jails led us to more questions and more discoveries. It brought us to a deeper understanding of New Brunswick's development.

This book is an illustrated journey through our home province, focussing on cultural and natural history. Readers will find familiar sites and favourite festivals in these pages; they will also find new destinations and events. We hope this book is an invitation to further exploration of all corners of New Brunswick.

We are thankful to the many people at the natural sites, museums and festivals for taking the time to explain the history and heritage behind the obvious. Thanks are also due to the historians and authors who have contributed their knowledge to the book: Richard Wilbur, Patrick Polchies, Jean-Roch Cyr, Benoit Bérubé, Wallace Brown, Harold Wright and George Peabody. A further credit goes to Andrée Bourque and other fine New Brunswickers who gave us their stories and shared valuable information. Last, but certainly not least, we'd like to express our gratitude to Jim Lorimer and Elizabeth Eve of Formac Publishing for their encouragement.

Marianne Eiselt

Saint-Jacques

The drive along the St. John River offers a 677-km (420-mi) stretch of water and some surprising changes of scenery, history and culture. The first surprise comes upon entering New Brunswick via Quebec's Highway 184 (the Trans-Canada route). This high country is home to 40,000 inhabitants of the mythical "Republic of Madawaska," which has its own coat of arms, a flag and the largest francophone festival east of Quebec. After the Treaty of Paris in 1783, the Madawaska region found itself in the middle of an international boundary dispute between Maine, Quebec and New Brunswick. While awaiting the boundary decision, the region had to be administered, the land parcelled out and forests explored and so it became a republic unto itself. To this day, this north-west corner of New Brunswick is distinct, yet the Madawaskans share a common heritage with thousands of other New Brunswickers.

In Saint-Jacques, along the scenic drive, you can take a

New Brunswick Botanical Garden, Saint-Jacques

stroll in the New Brunswick Botanical Garden, a centre of natural beauty. Spread out over seven hectares (18 acres), more than 50,000 plants are presented in several individual gardens. Small pathways lead through the rose garden, the shade garden and the alpine garden, which is planted on the ledges of a small waterfall. The New Brunswick Botanical Garden is indeed an oasis of colour, perfumes and music: Mozart among the roses, Handel in the rhododendrons...

An additional nearby attraction is the Antique Automobile Museum, featuring two floors of mint condition vehicles dating back to the turn of the century. One of the most intriguing exhibits is an 1899 Woods Electric Hanson cab. It looks like

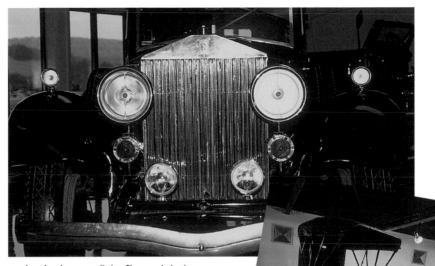

Saint-Jacques' Antique Automobile Museum

a horsedrawn wagon, has a top speed of 20 kmh (12 mph) and sold for $3,050, a huge sum when it was built. The Hanson ran on electricity, and a charge lasted for 40 miles. Another car that was perhaps ahead of its time was built right here in New Brunswick. The Bricklin is a fascinating vehicle, made of acrylic and fibreglass, so it won't rust. Other features include a steel-protected gasoline tank and gull-wing doors. But more than high technology and business, the story of the Bricklin is political. Malcolm Bricklin, a colourful Arizona entrepreneur, tried to get the Quebec government to invest in his plan to build a futuristic car, but he was unsuccessful. New Brunswick's premier, Richard Hatfield, jumped at the suggestion. New Brunswick's Bricklin plant opened in 1975, but after only 15 months and an $18 million-loss by the government, the Bricklin project died.

Motoring along the scenic drive brings you to Grand Falls, where the St. John River turns into a thunderous waterfall and plummets down a rock-sided ravine. Here, the water drops some 23 m (76 ft) to the bottom of the deep

Harvest display, New Brunswick Botanical Garden, Saint-Jacques

Grand Falls

gorge. The wooden stairway down to the "Wells in Rocks" allows a closer look at these large, circular depressions in the rocks, created by the erosive action of swirling water. Today, during the spring freshet, six million litres (1.3 million gallons) of water plunges down the falls every second. That's 90 percent of the volume of Niagara Falls. A short walk towards the dam on Lover's Lane takes visitors to an iron ring, a reminder of Evangeliste van Morrel, who, in 1904, walked across these falls on an iron cable. Photos of this daredevil act are included in an exhibit at the Grand Falls Museum.

A detour off the River Valley Scenic Drive on route 108 brings you to New Denmark. The names on the mailboxes are the first clue that this is a distinct community. Instead of McKinley, Kennedy and Duguay, you will see Pedersen, Hansen, Christiansen and Jensen. Also you'll begin to see red and white flags waving in the gentle breeze, but rather than the familiar maple leaf, their symbol is a white cross on a red background. You know that you have entered

"Danish territory" where Danish traditions are very much alive — especially in the village of New Denmark.

On Founders' Day (June 19), children perform traditional dances on a stage near a replica of the original Immigrant House. Children in red, white and black outfits dancing the Shoemaker's Dance and King Gustav Skol evoke the rich culture the Danes brought with them, which helped sustain them through the hardships they endured in the early years. The painting on the back wall of the stage depicts the original Immigrant House and the newly cleared land with just the tree stumps protruding from the ground.

The first settlers came in 1872, lured by the government's promise of 100 acres (40.5 hectares) of good farm land for every male over 18 years of age. It is thought that the government hoped the Danes, by forming a buffer between the English and the French, would serve to help reduce tension. Twenty-nine people, including 10 children, embarked on a steamer out of Copenhagen on May 31. When they arrived in Halifax, the Danes boarded a smaller boat and continued their journey to Saint John. Here, they boarded yet another vessel, which took them up the St. John River to Fredericton, where they transferred to a small paddle wheeler for a journey to the mouth of the Salmon River at Whitehead Flats. The final leg of the trip was a steep, rocky climb up a 3-km (2-mi) trail, now called Lucy Gulch. A Loyalist settler provided them with a team of horses. On June 19, 1872, they finally reached the spot on which the government-built Immigrant House stood. This is where they were to live until they could build their own homes. They were each provided with 100 acres of their own land, but farmland it was not! Dense forests covered the area and clearing the land was the first priority. Their feelings are recorded in a publication of the Women's Institute: "They had come from a country that resembled a gigantic garden…they were like children abandoned in the merciless woods."

Unfortunately, the original Immigrant House burned down. Only a smaller replica remains as a reminder of the rough early days. It is part of the New Denmark Museum, which is well worth a visit. Many historical photographs record the results of their hard work. Most Danes farmed near Klokkedahl Hill. If you continue past the museum and turn right onto the steep Lucy Gulch you will arrive at the settlers' landing site on the Salmon River, now a small picnic area.

Painting of Immigrant House, New Denmark Museum

Young women in traditional Danish costume

Hartland and Woodstock

Hartland Covered Bridge, a national historic site

From the high rolling hill country around Grand Falls and New Denmark down to Hartland is the potato farmers' kingdom. The farmers' neat, substantial houses line the highway on the River Valley Scenic Drive. In their yards lie machinery designed for one thing only — the potato; close by the road and often built into a hill as added protection against winter's blast is at least one storage barn, more often several; and everywhere vast potato fields stretch over hilly terrain overlooking the St. John River.

Amidst the pastoral beauty, nestled along the St. John River, lies the town of Hartland. It is home to the longest covered bridge in the world. The Hartland Covered Bridge, a national historic site since 1980, is 391 m (1,282 ft) long. It was originally built without a roof by a private company in 1901. Being a private venture, there was a toll: each pedestrian was charged 3 cents, a wagon with a single horse cost 6 cents, and a double team was charged 12 cents. In 1906, the government bought the bridge, and in 1920, when ice floes caused severe damage, major repair work

Carleton County Courthouse

Courthouse was sold for about $800 and used as a livestock barn. In 1960 the local Historical Society acquired the building and restored it to its original elegance. Inside, photographs depict the sorry state of the courthouse during the first half of the twentieth century. Today, the jury's room features an interesting display depicting the work of Tappan Adney. Born in 1868, he was a travel writer and journalist, artist, naturalist and authority on American Indians. Academics at Harvard and other institutions often sought his advice on Indian folklore and languages.

The town of Woodstock celebrates rural life in New Brunswick with its annual Old Home Week, featuring a parade, tractor pulls, agricultural displays and tasty treats. Woodstock's heritage is also alive in its fine nineteenth-century architecture. A walking tour around downtown gives a glimpse of former times. At 128 Connell is the Classic Revival mansion built in 1839 and owned by the honourable Charles Connell, who was a successful politician and postmaster until he took the incredible step of issuing an official five-cent stamp in his own image. This misguided ego trip caused such a commotion that he was forced to resign from public office. Today, the Carleton County Historical Society owns the property.

At 119 Chapel stands the Judge Jones House in Gothic Revival style. The pointed Gothic windows over the entrance create a distinctive character. The white and green house at the corner of St. James and Grover is the Dunbar House, built in 1874 in Victorian Gothic Revival style. Its many nooks and crannies give it a spooky look, the stuff of mysteries (or horror movies!). A wolf-like gargoyle over the central dormer smiles grotesquely down on all who pass below. For a good background on historic Woodstock homes, refer to Allison Connell's book *A View of Woodstock: Historic Homes of the Nineteenth Century.*

was necessary and the roof was added in order to preserve the wood as much as possible.

Legend has it that every young man in the horse-and-buggy days felt it his right to let his horse rest under a covered bridge while he stole a kiss from the girl beside him. To this day covered bridges are also called "kissing bridges." At last count, there were still about 70 covered bridges in New Brunswick, but every year more fall victim to decay, accident and vandalism. The magnificent Hartland Bridge remains the finest example of a gradually disappearing tradition.

From Hartland, the River Valley Scenic Drive leads south to the village of Upper Woodstock and to the town of

House in Upper Woodstock

Woodstock. On the approach to the Old Carleton County Courthouse in Upper Woodstock, there is a majestic white building with elegant columns in the Classic Revival style. This was a home for horses, cows, hens and pigs for no less than 50 years.

The Old County Courthouse was built in 1833, then extended in 1836. In 1909, the neighbouring town of Woodstock was growing faster and insisted on having its own courthouse. So, in 1911, the Old County

Statue in front of Potato House near Hartland

Kings Landing

Kings Landing Historical Settlement, just off the Trans-Canada Highway 37 km (23 mi) west of Fredericton on the banks of the St. John River, is a recreation of a nineteenth-century New Brunswick village. When the nearby Mactaquac Dam was constructed in 1963, a number of houses that otherwise would have been submerged in the head pond were transported to this site. Now, about 50 buildings and a nineteenth-century wooden boat form a living museum on a 121-hectare (300-acre) site.

This small settlement represents life in a community of predominantly American Loyalist settlers and their descendants.

The Loyalists were former residents of Britain's 13 American colonies, who fought for the British Crown under George III against George Washington and the creation of the United States. At the end of the American War of Independence (1775-1783), the loyal colonists, who had supported the losing side, went into exile. In 1783, a group

Kings Landing Historical Settlement

Ingraham house and garden, Kings Landing

of approximately 15,000 Loyalists arrived mostly from New York City to settle along the St. John River Valley as far north as Woodstock. In fact, these settlers founded both Saint John and Fredericton. The Loyalists were entitled to free land grants and other government help during their first three years in New Brunswick. With back-breaking labour, they cleared the forested lands along the St. John River for farming. Those who survived the harsh weather, in tents and drafty shelters, can be accurately described as the founders of New Brunswick: its creation from what used to be Nova Scotia in 1784 was largely the result of the petitions of Loyalist residents, who did not want their affairs run from Halifax. Furthermore, the Loyalists introduced an independent legal system to New Brunswick.

New Brunswick's Loyalists were a cross-section of colo-

nial society: farmers, labourers, tradesmen, artisans, merchants, lawyers and former army officers. By the dawn of the nineteenth century, the Loyalists, their descendants and immigrants from England, Scotland and Ireland had cultivated their new land and prospered on it. Kings Landing Historical Settlement is evidence of this.

Several Kings Landing buildings are among those built by first generation Loyalists or their children. The oldest one is a fancy octagonal privy built in the 1790s for the large Loyalist country estate of Chief Justice John Saunders. This noble outhouse, now located in the Ingraham dwelling complex, is a fitting memorial to Loyalist pretensions to grandeur.

The saltbox-style house, originally located on Westmorland Street in Fredericton, is one of the earliest houses on the site. This small dwelling was the childhood home of Loyalist Peter Fisher, who became a successful merchant and prominent New Brunswick author of the 1825 *Sketches of New Brunswick*.

The Hagerman House, built in the 1830s in the popular Neo-Classical style of that time, followed a local tradition of framing the house with hand-hewn timbers, post-and-beam style. The house, restored to its 1870 appearance, showcases beautiful furniture made by St. Stephen-based cabinetmaker John Warren Moore. In the elegant Victorian dining room, typically reserved for special occasions, Moore's craftsmanship includes the dining table, the china cabinet and the plant stand. Moore's fine work is also evident in the parlour, where the "Lady's" and "Gentleman's" chairs with their elegant cabriole legs, the large desk and the church-like Gothic glass doors catch the eye.

Another example of Neo-Classical symmetry is the home of Ira Ingraham, a New Brunswick-born child of Loyalist parents. His father had joined the American Regiment at the outset of the war, before leaving to settle along the St. John River Valley. Ira's sister Hannah gives an account of their initial hardship: "We lived in a tent at St. Anne's until father got a house ready." It was early winter when her father led them into the new house where "no floor" was laid, "no windows, no chimney, no door, but we had a roof at last...a good fire was blazing and mother had a big loaf of bread...." The family's condition improved and Ira and his brother John established a prosperous farm, tannery and leather working shop. The Ingraham House was built in 1840, where Ira, his wife Olive and three of their adult sons, a cousin and the unmarried Aunt Hannah, who presided over family life

and had a reputation for healing the sick, lived quite comfortably.

In its interior, the Ingraham House showcases the work of New Brunswick's famous furniture maker Thomas Nisbet, who came to New Brunswick from Scotland in 1813 and set up shop in Saint John. Nisbet's high quality furniture includes the large mahogany desk and four-poster bed, the sofa table and game table as well as the Regency-style sofa. These pieces are evidence of excellence, a reputation for which New Brunswick's furniture makers enjoyed in the nineteenth century. The most striking feature of the Ingraham estate is its Victorian flower garden with its profusion of scents and colours from early June to October. Many Loyalists planted flower gardens as soon as their houses were built because flowers were an important part of their lives.

The Jones House is quite different from the other homes, as it is built of stone. According to family legend, Thomas Jones was in the midst of building his house when he heard that his wife had just given birth to their first son. But Jones, perhaps concerned that his wife and newborn son would soon want to move into the new house, continued laying stone and putting in windows, never pausing to see his new family member. The Jones House, with its solid stone construction and rich interior decorations, reflects the lifestyle of wealthy Loyalist families of the nineteenth century. Thomas Jones was a Justice of the Peace, Captain and Paymaster in the Militia and an Anglican church warden.

The arrival of new immigrants in the 1830s produced a shift in the population of New Brunswick. The Loyalists now in their second and third generations were joined by settlers from the British Isles. The Killeen family was one of many hardy, industrious couples who fled poverty in Ireland, but the land they received was unproductive and thus their farms were marginal, barely feeding the family. The Killeen Cabin, built in 1825 of squared logs, is an example of the first houses built by immigrants. The furnishings are simple and sparse, as there was money only for necessities.

The St. John River and its tributaries provided the necessary waterpower to operate sawmills and grist mills. Kings Landing sawmill, operational today, offers a look at 1830s technology. Its saw cuts a foot a minute, so it would take about three quarters of an hour to saw a full-sized tree. At the nearby grist mill, dating from 1885, buckwheat is ground into bran and flour.

Other rural industries include the blacksmith shop, carpenter shop and printing office. The cooper was also important because he supplied barrels and casks used as shipping and storage containers of the pre-industrial era. Larger industries such as carriage and sleigh factories and sash and door factories were developed by mid-century. The C.B. Ross Sash and Door Factory, seen in replica at Kings Landing, displays the equipment used in building doors and windows in early industrial society.

The Parish School at Kings Landing, dating back to 1840, is a small building with simple desks and benches. The blackboard is literally made of wooden boards blackened with shellac and stove blacking. The Bible was the major book used by the schoolteachers, perhaps with additional books supplied by the pupils' parents. Students learned by memorization and repetition, and school work competed for time with farm and household work.

The government also provided for the Church of England congregations, but not to other denominations. Most of the Loyalist Tory elite were followers of the Church of England.

However, many New Brunswickers joined Baptist movements which became popular in the early nineteenth century. By mid-century, the Church of England had begun a revival under Bishop John Medley. St. Mark's Church in Kings Landing can trace back its origin to Medley's influence.

The King's Head Inn, an example of Classic Revival style, is representative of a St. John River Valley inn of 1855. Inns were essential in the nineteenth century, when travel by road or river was a slow affair. A common term for inns was "half-way houses," referring to breaking the journey at mid-point between home and destination. Taverns had to provide at least two beds to qualify for the governmental liquor licence. Beds were sometimes scarce, but food and drink were abundant: "Everything to satisfy a hungry man is here. Ham and eggs, fowl, venison of moose or deer (found within a hundred yards), pies, doughnuts, and the inevitable applesauce," wrote W.T. Baird in *Seventy Years of New Brunswick Life*. Today, travellers can still satisfy their hunger and thirst. The dining room of King's Head Inn serves delicious meals from authentic Victorian recipes and the tap room serves tasty ale.

Antique buggies

Fredericton

Legislative Assembly, Fredericton

Fredericton, the City of Elms, is bordered on one side by the St. John River. This transportation lifeline brought settlers to these fertile shores, and because of its distance from the ocean, was chosen by Governor Carleton in 1785 as the provincial capital. The town was named in honour of Prince Frederick, second son of George III. The Governor and his Loyalist supporters envisioned "a haven for the King's friends" — supported by the Church of England — with a university to prepare their sons for careers in government, the military or respectable professions such as law. Land was set aside for a university, a military compound and an Anglican church. Indeed, King's College was founded in 1785 by the United Empire Loyalists, and in 1859 reorganized into the nondenomina-

tional University of New Brunswick. From 1845 to 1853 Christ Church Cathedral, one of the first Anglican cathedrals in North America, was built according to the special wishes of Bishop John Medley.

Because of Fredericton's capital status and proximity to the American border, military personnel of the 57th, the 54th and the 104th Foot regiments were stationed here. Canada's oldest regular infantry regiment, the Royal Canadian Regiment, was raised in Fredericstown on December 21, 1883. Today, the Old Officers' Quarters, the Soldiers' Barracks, the Guard House and the Militia Arms Store are testimony to the army's importance to Fredericton's early history.

For much of the nineteenth and well into the twentieth century New Brunswick's capital city remained a quiet provincial backwater, its local politicians — many of them descendants of the Loyalists — seemingly more interested in keeping the status quo than in encouraging commercial growth. They learned little from the success of "Boss" Alexander Gibson, who created and ran Marysville, across the river, where his cotton mill was one of Canada's largest in 1885. Marysville, now a part of Fredericton, has a large brick cotton mill at the banks of the Nashwaak River. Since 1985 the large building has undergone major restoration for office use by the provincial government. To this day, the

One of Fredericton's main architectural attractions is city hall. Erected in 1876 at the corner of Queen and York streets, it is the oldest city hall still in use in the Maritime provinces. In recent years, however, interior renovations and exterior restoration of the original building were undertaken to bring it in line with current standards. The old building once included the City office, council chamber, magistrate's office, jail, farmers' market and even an opera house. The tower clock with its eight-foot dials, copper hands and reliable chimes has been keeping Frederictonians on time since 1876.

The fountain in front of city hall features Fredericton's very own "Freddy, the nude dude," as he is affectionately called. City hall's

Officers' Square, Fredericton (top)
School museum (below)

former company town showcases streets lined with rows of bygone brick workers' tenements, ornate managers' homes and stores. What the industrious and well-respected Boss Gibson began as a modest mill operation, became a prosperous town, and most of the town's workers were employed at the mill.

During the First and Second World Wars, Fredericton was the site of a basic training centre for the Canadian Armed Forces. In the 1950s, Canada's largest peacetime army base, Camp Gagetown, opened in nearby Oromocto, thereby bolstering the local economy.

In 1973, Fredericton amalgamated several surrounding communities, doubling its size and its population to 45,000. The people and events that changed Fredericton from a settlement in the wilderness into an administrative and educational centre have also left their cultural influences on the city. Fredericton has managed to retain its Loyalist flavour, thanks to the existence of such amenities as Odell Park and the gracious architecture. Along the tree-lined streets dwell gifted artists and craftspeople, as well as recognized scholars and scientists.

opera house ceased operation in the 1940s, and with the construction of Boyce Market on George Street in 1952, the farmers' market found a new home. But city hall was still crowded and plans were made for an administrative extension, keeping intact the character of a building that is so much a part of the city's past. In 1985, a portrait of Prince Frederick, the city's namesake, was hung in council chamber. Here, the last 200 years of Fredericton are permanently displayed in a series of unique tapestries by artisans Gertrude Duffie and Dr. Ivan H. Crowell.

One block east of city hall on Queen Street is Officers' Square and the Officers' Quarters, one of the garrison city's most beautiful and historic areas. During the summer, there is an hourly ceremony of the changing of the guard and performances at the outdoor theatre. The Officers' Quarters

Highland Games, Fredericton

building facing the Parade Square represents an architectural style typical of the colonial period: stone arches, iron handrails and staircase. Today, the building houses the York-Sunbury Historical Society Museum featuring New Brunswick aboriginal, domestic and military history. There is a pioneer kitchen with many tools from a bygone age and a "what'zit" board that displays some of the more exotic implements. You can try your skill guessing what these tools were used for. On the top floor you'll find what this museum is most famous for: the 42-pound Coleman frog.

Further east on Queen Street is the majestic Provincial Legislative Assembly Building, an impressive sandstone structure in Second Empire style. It has been the seat of government since 1882. A guided tour of this elegant building passes through hallways lined with pictures of former lieutenant-governors, into the legislative chamber. In a cabinet the mace is displayed. The mace — the traditional sign of power — is placed next to the table in the chamber whenever the house is in session. One of the most impressive elements in the beautifully decorated assembly

chamber is the Throne or Speaker's Chair under a canopy bearing the carving of the Royal Coat-of-Arms. It serves as the Throne when the Lieutenant-Governor enters the chamber, and during the legislative sessions, it is the Speaker's Chair. The chamber is decorated in late Victorian style. The fancy wallpaper is Japanesque, the carpet from England is in traditional green and the chandeliers are made of brass with crystal prisms.

The tour continues by climbing part of the 12-m (40-ft) free-standing (and slightly sloping) spiral staircase. Its fancy woodwork includes walnut, cherry, ash and pine. Upstairs, from the visitors' gallery, there is a view down to the elegant chamber. Back on the main floor is the Legislative Library, with its treasured volume of 435 hand-coloured copper engravings of John James Audubon's *Birds of America*. The oversized book with Audubon's plates of birds from 1820 is permanently displayed in the building. As the plates would deteriorate under the influence of light, they are kept covered except for viewing. The monetary value of Audubon's book these days was evident at a Christie's auction in the year 2000, where a copy sold for $8.8 million — a record sale price for a single book.

Across from the Legislative Assembly is the Beaverbrook Art Gallery, a gift from Lord Beaverbrook, the declared "native son of New Brunswick," who was raised in New Brunswick, built a publishing empire and served Britain as

Carriage House Inn

Minister of Aircraft Production during the Second World War. The famous gallery houses a prestigious collection of British paintings by Thomas Gainsborough, J. M. W. Turner and John Constable. The impressive, oversized "Santiago el Grande," by Salvador Dali, is permanently on display. The gallery also has an extensive permanent collection of paintings by Cornelius Krieghoff, among them the celebrated "Merrymaking." In the permanent collection are also works of art by the Group of Seven, Emily Carr and David Milne. The gallery also features a variety of travelling exhibitions, some period furniture and china.

With a clear view of the Beaverbrook Art Gallery is Crocket House, another Fredericton landmark. It houses Gallery 78, one of New Brunswick's oldest commercial galleries, representing distinguished Canadian artists and artisans such as Molly Lamb and Bruno Bobak, Tom Forrestall, Cheryl Bogart, Michael Khoury, Gordon Dunphy and Mary and Christopher Pratt.

On "The Green," the local name for the park along the bank of the St. John River, is a fine-looking statue of Robert Burns, which was erected by the municipal and provincial Scottish societies in 1906. Nearby is a marble fountain from Buckinghamshire, England, which Lord Beaverbrook placed on The Green in memory of his friend Sir James Dunn, also from New Brunswick.

Opposite is Christ Church Cathedral, a national historic site since 1983. Construction of the massive church began in 1845, modelled after a medieval church in England and built under the strong influence of Bishop John Medley. The natural stone used for its construction was quarried in New Brunswick, and most of the woodwork, such as the wainscot panelling along both sides of the nave, is made of butternut, adding character and atmosphere to this impressive cathedral.

The Green River Walk passes under the railroad bridge and continues on past beautiful homes in various architectural styles, such as the stately house at 58 Waterloo Row, now the residence of the president of the University of New Brunswick. Since its transformation into a foot bridge as part of the TransCanada Trail network in 1997, the CN

Fredericton's gracious homes

Railway bridge stretching over the St. John River is a favourite place for Frederictonians to stroll and enjoy views back to the city.

A special weekend of Scottish cultural entertainment is staged yearly on the grounds of the old Government House, a newly renovated building that serves as the seat of office for New Brunswick's Lieutenant-Governor and is also a national and provincial historic site.

The two-day Highland Games pay tribute to the Maritimes' Scottish ancestry. This cultural event dates back to the fateful battle of Culloden in 1746, when thousands of Highlanders lost their lives. In order to retain their cultural identity, some Scots joined the British army or emigrated to Canada, mainly to the Maritimes and Upper Canada.

The annual Highland Games feature dancing, piping and drumming competitions, massed bands and heavyweights events, the latter including "putting the weight over the bar," "throwing the hammer" and, most famously, "tossing the caber." The caber is a 7-m (20-ft), 66 kg (150-pound) pole that must be flipped over by the athlete. If the piping, drumming and the athletic events leave visitors hungry or thirsty, they can enjoy Scottish fare, such as haggis and Irn-Bru, a typical Scottish soft drink, or the traditional afternoon tea with freshly baked scones and other homemade sweets.

Lower St. John River Valley

St. John River Valley

The lower St. John River Valley is a large watershed dotted with charming peninsulas, islands and quaint villages that are served by small ferries. More than half a dozen ferries operate toll-free for the public across the St. John River and its tributaries.

One of these ferries across the river operates from Gagetown, a community with a distinctly artistic flavour: among the artists who have

St. John River ferry at Gagetown

made Gagetown their home are Flo Greig, Enid Inch, Peter Thomas and Karen Shackleton.

The main road on the shores of the St. John River is lined with craft shops, artists' studios, coffee shops, a gallery, a marina, the fine Steamer's Stop Country Inn and Sir Leonard Tilley's boyhood home. Now a museum, this gracious home is where Sir Leonard Tilley, who became one of Canada's Fathers of Confederation, was born on May 18, 1818. A costumed guide welcomes visitors to the 13-room house. The Loyalist kitchen features a huge fireplace, built with hand-made bricks. Here you'll also find two machines that roll thread from a spinning wheel into yarn — a "squirrel cage," and a "weasel." The latter is an innovative design: the turning

Tilley House, Gagetown

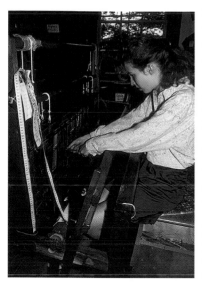

Gagetown loomcrofters

motion rolls the thread onto a gear with a small pin on the side. When the gear completes one revolution, a wooden lever, pushed forward by the pin, flaps back with a popping noise — hence the children's song "Pop! Goes the Weasel." Another room in the house served originally as the office of Dr. Stickles, who built this house in 1786, though it looks more like a torture chamber than a doctor's office.

At the top of the original pine stairs, there is a cozy children's room with a spool bed, as well as a fancy spruce gum box and a gramophone with cylinder records. There are also some fine Mi'kmaq baskets. The wide wooden floorboards were repainted 30 years ago with paint made according to a time-honoured recipe: one plug of tobacco mixed with one pint of ammonia produces the reddish colour seen here.

The Gagetown loomcrofters are housed in a small studio built in 1761 as a farm outbuilding. About 60 years ago, it was moved to its present location in the peaceful St. John River Valley. In the tiny showroom, two loomcrofters typically work on place mats, table runners, boys' and men's tartan ties or tartan afghans. This isn't mass production — it takes about four days to weave an afghan. The traditional craft of weaving became popular in Gagetown thanks to the late designer, weaver and teacher Patricia Jenkins. In 1940, Mrs. Jenkins created the official Royal Canadian Air Force tartan, and in the 1950s, she designed the official New Brunswick tartan.

Sussex, the dairy centre of New Brunswick, is also home to the annual Atlantic Balloon Fiesta.

Back in 1986, several prominent local businesspeople wanted to attract visitors to Sussex in the off-season. They invited some maritime balloonists to Sussex for a fall weekend and the fiesta was born. It now includes a craft show and an antique car show held on the weekend after Labour Day.

Another attraction is the New Brunswick Agricultural Museum, located at the western side of the Balloon Launch Site. A huge threshing machine, the "Little Giant," was actually made right in Sussex. The museum offers theme rooms, depicting rural life of bygone times. Of specific interest is the huge collection of oil lamps and tools — from log hooks, adzes and a surveyor's chain for measuring distances, to one of the first milking machines. An old train station and circular black markings on the original hardwood floors remind us where the milk cans stood, before they got to market — by train.

Agricultural Museum, Sussex (right)

Atlantic Balloon Fiesta

Campobello Island

Bay of Fundy from Campobello Island

The 450-km (281-mi) Fundy Coastal Drive offers a variety of incredible natural phenomena. Indeed the Bay of Fundy, that remarkable body of tidal water, has shaped New Brunswick's southern shoreline. There is nothing quite like the bay anywhere else in the marine world. Its full-moon tides can reach 8.5 m (28 ft). Its many whirlpools and swirling currents act as giant pumps bringing in a mixture of tiny marine organisms that in turn lure all kinds of creatures: from schools of herring and mackerel to bluefin tuna, minke, humpback or right whales.

It was these marine riches that first drew humans to the Bay of Fundy's shores. From the earliest times, aboriginals harvested clam beds and caught herring and salmon in weirs. The first European settlement attempt took place over the winter of 1604-5 when an ill-fated expedition led by Samuel de Champlain encamped on the tiny St. Croix Island. After an unusually severe winter and a scurvy epidemic, the expedition retreated to the other side of the bay, to a site they called Port Royal, now in Nova Scotia.

Closer to the Maine border lies the island of Campobello. It remained the feudal fief of a dynasty of Welsh seamen until the late 1800s, among them Captain William Owen, who established a settlement there in 1770. The Owen family sold most of their property in 1881 to a Boston realty firm. One shoreline lot was bought by the Delano family, whose daughter married a Roosevelt. Their son, Franklin Delano Roosevelt, better known as FDR, spent most of his boyhood summers here in a big cottage that has become Campobello's major tourist attraction. Connected to Lubec, Maine, by a highway bridge, Campobello had a strong American link back in the early twentieth century.

Roosevelt Cottage, Campobello Island

On the ground floor of the Hubbards' house there is a bright and airy living room furnished in light oak. The dining room is notable not so much for its furniture as its unusual oval window and the beautiful view it offers of the bay.

These cottages are by no means the only attractions on Campobello Island. The Roosevelt Campobello International Park and the adjacent Herring Cove Provincial Park both have scenic hiking trails along the coast, to a bog and through shaded woodlands. Aside from hiking, visitors to the island spend time golfing, beachcombing and whale watching. A trip to the Head Harbour Lighthouse at the northern tip of the island is well worthwhile. The view from the lighthouse complex — accessible only at low tide — is breathtaking.

This continues to the present-day: the island is a favourite vacation place for wealthy Americans.

The Roosevelt Cottage, a misnomer if there ever was one, is a stately home with 34 rooms on 1.6 hectares (4 acres) of land, with a fine view of the Bay of Fundy. A tour of the red and green house offers a glimpse of Roosevelt the individual. As a little boy all he wanted for Christmas, he wrote to his mother, was "a box of blocks, and a train, and a little boat." During a summer vacation in August 1921, Roosevelt developed what was diagnosed as a severe cold after fighting a forest fire, and then taking a dip in the icy waters of the bay. A month later, after he was partially paralysed, his condition was diagnosed as polio. After that, he returned a few times to the island. He served as president of the United States from 1933 to 1945.

An international park (jointly administered by Canada and the United States) was established on the property in 1964. The Hubbards, friends of the Roosevelts, have a summer home nearby. Mr. Hubbard was an insurance broker from Boston.

St. Stephen

St. Stephen, a small town on the American border, is situated along the western end of the Fundy Coastal Drive. St. Stephen is best known for chocolates and chicken bone candies. Once a year, in early August, the town hosts the International Chocolate Festival, sponsored and initiated mainly by the Ganong Chocolate Factory.

A good way to begin to explore the town is with a visit to the Charlotte County Museum on Milltown Boulevard. The museum is housed in the 1864 dwelling of the prominent lumberman James Murchie. It showcases the history, domestic and social life as well as the industrial development of the area from its Loyalist beginnings. Not surprisingly, there is a Ganong Chocolates room in the museum, showcasing some of the old chocolate bar moulds, traditional chocolate packages from 1909 and 1920 and some historic Ganong streetcar signs — "With Ganong

Chocolate Festival, St. Stephen

chocolate, no lady can refuse you." Within reason, this is probably still true to this day.

Ganong candy and chocolate production has a long and illustrious tradition here. Founded in 1873 by James and Gilbert Ganong, the factory is Canada's oldest candy manufacturer. One of the world's favourite treats — the chocolate bar — was reputedly created here in 1910, and in the 1930s chocolate-filled heart-shaped boxes, designed for Valentine's Day, captured the market. And kept it! More chocolates are sold on February 14 than any other day of the year.

Spots on the popular tours that are conducted only during the few days of the Chocolate Festival have to be reserved in advance. These "sweetheart" tours are organized like clockwork: every few minutes a new group of guests exchanges tickets for white caps, compulsory attire inside the plant. The group enters the building with a guide who leads visitors

Ganong Chocolate Factory, St. Stephen

turning out the ever-popular jelly bean, which is no less than eight days in the making! At the next stop, almond candies are hand-dipped. Last, but certainly not least, visitors are invited to sample some of the factory's products: from chocolate-covered burnt almonds and orange fondant to vanilla frappé and cream toffee. And then there are the wintergreen lozenges, jelly beans, spearmint leaves and chicken bone candies. On the way out, visitors receive

through the supply room and past a machine shop to the Lozenges Room, with its nineteenth-century machinery.

This is the "birthplace" of wintergreen lozenges and double thick mints. In the next room, candies are dipped into chocolate, a pattern is sprayed on top in chocolate, and the shiny round goodies are put in a dryer for about 15 minutes. They are manually inspected, and, if not perfect, are sent back. A sweet tip for chocoholics is that the rejects are later dipped again and sold as "double-dips" — cheaper, but with almost twice as much chocolate! In yet another room a dozen or so large cauldrons are constantly turning — and

coupons for mint candies, redeemable in the Ganong store in town, further sweetening the deal.

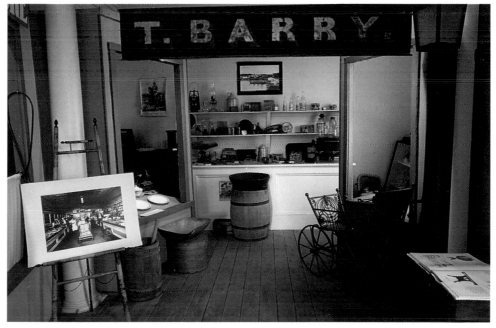

Charlotte County Museum, St. Stephen

St. Andrews

Fairmont Algonquin hotel, St. Andrews-by-the-Sea

Along the Fundy Coastal Drive lies the town of St. Andrews-by-the-Sea, one of the country's most beautiful seaside resorts. Once a haven for United Empire Loyalists fleeing the American Revolution in 1783, St. Andrews remains steeped in traditional charm and luxurious accommodations.

Boasting "No hay fever and a railway" in the late nineteenth century, gracious hotels were built to make St. Andrews the first choice in Canadian resorts. The Algonquin, New Brunswick's most famous resort hotel and a town landmark, was built by local businessmen. In 1902, Sir William Van Horne and Sir Thomas Shaughnessy, two American-born industrialists who rose to fame and fortune in Montreal as heads of the Canadian Pacific Railway Company, bought the stylish Tudor Revival hotel and created a booming tourist town. Van Horne also purchased Minister's Island, now a provincial historic site accessible from St. Andrews at low tide, where he built a grand

Water Street, St. Andrews-by-the-Sea

The heart of downtown is Water Street. As the name suggests, it runs parallel to the shore. Water Street is lined with craft shops, galleries, boutiques, coffee shops, an internet café, fine restaurants and quaint inns.

All the downtown stores were designed to fit in with the architectural heritage — among them a gas station, a garage and a supermarket.

Just a few steps off Water Street on King is Sheriff Andrews' House, built in 1820 by Elisha Shelton Andrews, sheriff of Charlotte County and son of the Loyalist Reverend Samuel Andrews. Nine period-furnished rooms with working fireplaces tell of middle-class domestic life in a seaport town in the early nineteenth century. Sheriff Andrews had seven children and two servants; the latter lived in the servants' quarters on the third floor, reached by a separate staircase. A drawing room on the ground floor contains a strongbox, undoubtedly for the sheriff's documents. Three leather fire buckets hang on pegs in the hallway, as required by law. In the basement is a large "keeping room" with a shallow fireplace, specially designed to give off more heat than a deeper one would. During the summer season, museum guides bake biscuits in the "beehive oven."

Nearby, on the corner of King and Montague streets, is the Ross Memorial Museum, a neoclassical brick building

summer residence, a circular bath house and tidal swimming pool and an impressive barn for his prize Dutch cattle. Shaughnessy stayed near the Algonquin in a retreat called Fort Tipperary, which still bears the name today. Both men had international connections that were soon reflected in the Algonquin's clientele. The business and social elite of Boston, New York and Montreal helped establish the hotel and the town. Today, the Fairmont Algonquin is a "Castle by-the-Sea" that features exquisite accommodation, fine dining and a wealth of recreational facilities — including the signature 18-hole ocean view golf course.

The town's core has been designated a national historic district and several homes — some over 200 years old — have been marked with descriptive plaques. The renowned architects Edward and W.S. Maxwell of Montreal built many of these gracious summer homes in the nineteenth century. Some of the older homes came from Castine, Maine, where early settlers dismantled them and shipped them aboard barges to St. Andrews. Here they were reassembled and can still be seen today.

St. Andrews' streets follow the traditional grid pattern, with street names such as King, Queen, Elizabeth, William and Princess Royal, signifying the town's Loyalist heritage.

Town wharf, St. Andrews

The Charlotte County Court House and Gaol, built in 1840, is now a national historic site. It is New Brunswick's best preserved example of a typical mid-nineteenth-century courthouse and jail. The hand-carved royal coat of arms in the pediment was an artistic flourish added in 1858. Visitors are often impressed by the cell area, its atmosphere and the harsh criminal justice system of the

time. The jail now houses the recorded history of Charlotte County.

The St. Andrews' town wharf, just off Water Street, has long been a working wharf for scallop draggers, fishing boats and aquaculture barges. From here, visitors can head out into the Passamaquoddy Bay aboard a cutter, catamaran cruiser or racing Zodiac to watch whales. Touring the harbour in a sea kayak is another exciting adventure. The Huntsman Marine Science Centre and Aquarium/Museum is named after Dr. Huntsman (1883-1973), who stimulated fishery research in the region. One of the attractions of the centre is the three harbour seals who are fed herring twice a day. Displays include a fossilized molar tooth of a woolly mammoth (from the Passamaquoddy Bay) and a variety of fish, snakes and frogs of the area. In the "Touch Pool"

*Kingsbrae Garden,
St. Andrews*

first occupied in 1824 by the Honourable Harris Hatch. The minister, Henry Phips Ross, and his wife, Sarah Juliette, daughter of the president of an important financier, bought the house in 1938. Their pictures grace the chandelier-lit hallway of the home. Thanks to Mrs. Ross's large inheritance, the couple travelled widely, returning each year with rare treasures in fine furniture, crystal and carpets. The "Morning Room" showcases an 1810 piano. The spacious dining room contains massive mahogany furniture, including two writing desks and a bookcase. A spiral staircase leads to the white and peach master bedroom with a round table beautifully inlaid with mother-of-pearl, soapstone, jade and other semi-precious stones.

Sea kayaking, St. Andrews

Touch pool at Huntsman Marine Centre

visitors can actually touch starfish, sea urchins, sea cucumbers and giant scallops.

Not far from the Huntsman Marine Centre is St. Andrews' Blockhouse, erected as a coastal border defense during the war of 1812 and now a national historic site, administered by the federal government. It was built by townspeople in fear of an American invasion. This is one of 12 existing blockhouses in St. Andrews. They were quickly constructed, using local squared timber to form a structure about 6 metres square on the lower floor — the upper storey overhung almost a metre on each side. The sturdiness of this construction rendered them relatively secure against attack. In addition to the side gun ports and loopholes, holes were cut in the floor of the overhang to cover besiegers directly below.

St. Andrews' most recent attraction is the enchanting Kingsbrae Garden (Scottish for Kings Hill Garden), a 10-hectare site located at the top of the town overlooking Minister's Island and Passamaquoddy Bay. The estate and property that form the garden were donated by John and Lucinda Flemer. Traditionally, the estate had beautiful gardens, and the Kingsbrae Garden expands this heritage. Opened in 1998, it now features more than 40,000 plants and flowers in a variety of garden settings and themes such as the Cottage Garden, Knot and Rose Garden, Bird and Butterfly Garden, Therapy Garden, Touch and Feel Garden and the Children's Garden. The horticultural showcase also features a cedar maze, two ponds, streams and a fully functioning windmill. The Acadian Forest trail leads visitors among trees of the coastal region. The Garden Café, overlooking a park with a fountain and modern statues, offers culinary delights which can be enjoyed out on the patio or inside out of the sun. The Kingsbrae Gardens was recently named one of Canada's top 10 public gardens.

St. Andrews' Blockhouse

Grand Manan

Grand Manan, the "Queen of the Fundy Isles," has long been a haven for summer residents, both Canadian and American. But possibly the island's first visitors were Passamaquoddy Indians collecting eggs of gulls and other seabirds. They called it *man an ook,* meaning "island place." In 1604, the French explorer Samuel de Champlain recorded seeking shelter here during a storm. He added the term "Grand" to "Manan," a French adaptation of the original Indian name. Subsequently, the island changed hands a number of times between the French and the English, reflecting the fortunes of

Grand Manan

war on the faraway continent. In 1784, fifty United Empire Loyalist families arrived, and many of today's residents are descendants of these Loyalists. For a time it was unclear whether Britain or the newly independent United States owned the island. The boundary dispute was finally settled in 1842 in favour of the British.

Grand Manan's natural beauty and solitude has attracted naturalists, geologists, writers and artists over the last 200 years. The visit of John James Audubon to Grand Manan in the mid-nineteenth century has resulted in hundreds of birders coming to the island to look for rare birds among the 250 species that nest here. The feature exhibit in the museum on Grand Manan pays tribute to naturalist and taxidermist Allan Moses (1881-1953), whose superb collection includes a snowy owl, egrets, mergansers, teals, plovers and falcons.

Dr. Abraham Gesner conducted a geological survey on the island in 1839 and reported that the eastern area consists of very old sedimentary rock, whereas the western part is formed by much younger volcanic rock. The line where the two geological formations meet is clearly visible in the cliff face at Red Point beach.

The American Buchanan Charles of North Andover, Massachusetts, founded the Grand Manan Historical Society in 1931 and his remarkable collection of historical material was later donated to the society's archives. The American author Willa Cather (*O, Pioneers!*) is one of the well-known writers who once called the island home.

Grand Manan, at the mouth of the Bay of Fundy, is wedge-shaped. The western shore is a sheer cliff more than 100 m (100 yd) in height and running the full 25-km (16-mi) length of the island. In contrast, the eastern side has a

Grand Manan seaweed processing at a lobster pound

A large bundle of dried dulse

low contour, and is sheltered by other small islands. All the villages and roads are found on this protected eastern shore. Basically, there is a wilderness with high, forbidding cliffs on one side, spruce forest, streams and wetlands in the middle and a strip of settlement, going back almost 220 years, on the eastern side.

Many of the hiking trails that wind along the western cliff tops once served as life-saving paths — the number of shipwrecks around the island gave rise to a patrol and rescue path. Six lighthouses guard the archipelago against the dangerous ledges that stretch across the bay to the south and west. Visible only from the Southwest Head Light, and 1.5 km (.9 mi) out in the Bay of Fundy, the Gannet Rock Lighthouse has stood as guardian since 1831. A year later, a second lighthouse was erected at Machias Seal Island, located about a half-hour boat ride off Grand Manan, to guard the other end of the shipping hazard. Both New Brunswick and Maine claim Machias Seal Island; today the island is administered jointly. The island's puffin colony has drawn so many birders over the years that it was decided to limit access. Now a single group of Canadian visitors can spend the morning there, while the afternoon is reserved for a boatload of birdwatchers out of Eastport, Maine.

Swallowtail Lighthouse at North Head, Grand Manan, is located on a peninsula that offers spectacular views of herring weirs, fishing boats and sea birds. Every two hours, the ferry from the mainland can be seen as it rounds the peninsula.

Seining of the weirs can also be watched at Whale Cove. The Jubilee Weir is visible from the Hole-in-the-Wall, the picturesque natural arch at the edge of a cliff near the old airstrip. The herring are cured and packed for market at the smoked herring plant and at Connor's Sardine Factory right on the island. Grand Manan boasts some of the finest smoked herring in the world and packing sardines into cans has been a mainstay of the local economy for many years. Due to the steady flushing action of the tides, Grand Manan has a lobster pound, where lobsters are kept in captivity until they are ready for market.

Dark Harbour, one of the most scenic parts of the island, is known for its dulse, an edible reddish-purple seaweed, which is harvested at low tide, then spread out on a net on crushed rock to dry. On a sunny day, it dries in about five hours. The dulse leaves then stick to each other and the harvest can be rolled like carpet. It first goes into storage, then is ground into flakes or powder. While chewing it raw is an acquired taste, it is also widely used as seasoning on fish, eggs and potato salad. The natural lagoon at Dark Harbour is also used for trout and salmon aquaculture ventures. The imposing cliffs, scenic views and breathtaking sunsets make Dark Harbour a must see.

Swallowtail Peninsula

Saint John

"Three Sisters," lamppost, Saint John

Saint John, Canada's first incorporated city, is situated where the mighty St. John River meets the force of the Bay of Fundy tides. The city's site was once a traditional gathering place and village for nomadic Maliseet Indians. Samuel de Champlain marked this place on his map after meeting the Indians and their chief on his short visit on June 24, 1604. Today, a statue of Samuel de Champlain in Queen's Square memorializes his arrival and naming of the town almost 400 years ago.

After the French lost possession of this region, the English erected Fort Howe, perched high above the city near the former homes of James Simonds and James White, two successful Boston merchants who had settled here in the 1760s. Constructed in 1777 in Halifax, Fort Howe was later disassembled and rebuilt at Saint John to protect the harbour from American privateers and hostile Indians. Within a year, all raids had stopped, and from 1785 on, the blockhouse served as the city's first jail. Today, the small fort is locked, but the grounds offer a panoramic view of the city and port.

The harbour witnessed the arrival of many frigates, "but never in its renowned and varied history did it behold such a scene as on May 11, 1783, when a number of little sailing craft winged their way up the Bay of Fundy, rounded Partridge Island, and dropped anchor to the salute of guns from Fort Howe," wrote historian H.A. Cody, describing the arrival of Loyalist refugees. From May to September 1783, more than 2,000 Loyalists arrived at the mouth of the St. John River. They had fled their homes in the 13 colonies at the end of the Revolutionary War, fearing prosecution for their loyalty to the Crown.

During Loyalist Days, the city annually remembers the arrival of exiled Loyalists by

Festival by the Sea in Saint John

Exhibit at the Firefighters' Museum, Saint John

In response to the fire and two years after Saint John was incorporated as a city in 1787, a system of fire protection was established. Wells were sunk and two fire engines purchased. This was the era of the hand pump — the first phase in mechanized firefighting. One of these old hand pumpers, a wagon with two long handles on its sides, is on display in the Firefighters' Museum on King's Square. During a fire, six volunteers were stationed at each handle; they were able to operate two pistons that pumped the water through two hoses.

Loyalist Days at Saint John Market Slip

re-enacting the landing at Market Slip next to Market Square. Spectators line the pier to welcome the boats carrying King's Royals in period costumes. The entourage climbs up the pier and, accompanied by a guard, heads down to the open-air auditorium facing Market Square to begin the week-long festival with the mayor's opening speech, music, prayers, a sweetgrass ceremony — traditionally conducted by local Indians so as to ensure that no falsehood was spoken in meetings — the raising of the flag and the cutting of the cake.

In 1783, as soon as Saint John's streets were laid out, the Loyalists began to build their homes. King's Square and Queen's Square were reserved as public places. The walkways across the squares formed the pattern of the Union Jack, which is still evident today. Several stores and houses were built between King's Square and the Public Landing, now Market Square, but on June 18, 1784, a fire destroyed many of the buildings.

Trinity Church, Saint John

The Firefighters' Museum also features pictures of the Great Fire that destroyed two-thirds of Saint John in 1877. This disastrous conflagration rendered 2,700 families homeless. Old Trinity Church, Saint John's first Anglican church, which opened for use on Christmas Day, 1791, was destroyed in the Great Fire. During many years of reconstruction of the city, the church was replaced with the present Trinity Church in 1880 on its Germain Street location. The royal coat of arms, which survived the fire, is mounted over the west door. Today, Trinity Church is a national historic site. The Centenary Methodist Church, built in 1839 as a monument to a hundred years of Methodism, was also destroyed in the Great Fire. The present gothic structure, the largest church sanctuary in Saint John, was built on the same site on Wentworth Street in 1882. The

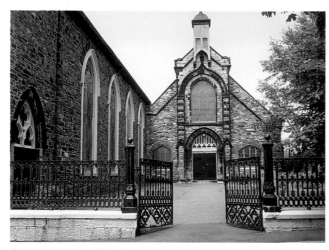

Saint John's Stone Church

Martello Tower, Saint John

newly named Centenary-Queen's Square United Church, resulting from a merger of two congregations in the 1950s, has a fine interior with 13 stained-glass windows. The most prominent, the Great South Window, is 6 m (20 ft) wide and 12 m (40 ft) high.

Unlike practically all the houses of the late 18th and early nineteenth century in downtown Saint John, the Loyalist House, completed in 1817, was not destroyed by the Great Fire. This Georgian-style home of David Merritt, located on a corner lot of Germain and Union Streets, is the oldest house in Saint John. The Loyalist House was acquired by the New Brunswick Historical Society in 1960. With municipal and provincial assistance the house was restored and opened as a museum. The house is meticulously furnished and decorated in a period no later than 1833, featuring rare artistry that was no longer crafted after the advent of mass produced furniture of the later Victorian era. The beautiful doors in the hallway are curved, which required careful steaming of the wood. The piano is more than it first appears; pull the right knob, push the appropriate pedal, and it becomes an organ. This Lemuel Gilbert piano with

Gargoyles on Stone Church

organ attachment is very rare. Another deceptive item is the commode of bird's eye maple. It has a decorative façade of false drawers. The entire top folds back, and there is the chamber pot! There is a Bible on the sewing table in the living room. Sunday was supposed to be the day of rest, but the sewing still had to be done. When the preacher came, the clothes went into the bag hanging from the table, the Bible was opened and everything was in order.

St. John's Stone Church, another surviving structure of the Great Fire, dates back to 1824. Its stained-glass windows were imported from England, Germany and

Toronto. Upstairs are the original pews and outside, high up on the tower, are 32 gargoyles whose faces are said to represent the builders of the church.

When the War of 1812 broke out and relations between Great Britain and the United States were strained, defensive measures were undertaken. Far on the west side of the city on a rocky knoll the mighty Carleton Martello Tower, a circular stone fortification, was erected. By the time the tower was finished the war was over, and hundreds of freed slaves from the southern States sought refuge on British ships and were brought to the city.

The Carleton Martello Tower has four floors. The interior of the round structure consists of a single room with

Saint John townhouses

a large supporting pillar in the centre. Along the brick walls are the bedsteads of the soldiers, complete with folding cot, mattress, pegs for their scarlet uniforms, canteen, and firearms. The basement is a heavily constructed powder

Synagogue, Saint John

storeroom. To reduce the risk of explosions, the only source of light was a single lantern. The site offers a spectacular view of the city, the harbour and the Bay of Fundy.

After the Napoleonic wars, waves of Scottish and Irish immigrants arrived, bringing artisan skills and religious diversity with them. The Irish potato famine in the 1840s brought thousands of destitute people to Saint John, many of them dying from typhus or the terrible conditions they endured on the passage. During the spring and summer of 1847, more than 16,000 passed through the quarantine station at Partridge Island at the harbour's entrance. More than a thousand were buried in mass graves.

Over the years, Partridge Island, a short boat ride from Saint John, became the equivalent of Ellis Island in New York Harbour. From 1785 to 1942, three million immigrants landed here, many from Eastern Europe. Their first impression must have been a wet and smelly one: they were first deloused with a kerosene shower, followed by a hot-water shower to take away the oily smell. In the meantime their belongings were steam-cleaned. The small museum on the island displays pictures of the immigrants' plight, suffering and survival. Two thousand Irish died here of typhus fever. They were treated by a dedicated young physician who himself fell victim to the disease. Most survivors headed for the "Boston States," but some stayed in Saint John or moved up the St. John River Valley to settle there. On the grounds of the small island, a Celtic cross commemorates the fever victims and Dr. Collins. Near the beach, a neatly fenced in area is a graveyard with three partitions: one for Protestants, one for Catholics and one for Jews.

In 1858, the first Jewish family arrived in Saint John; by 1898 the community had grown significantly and a synagogue was built. A second wave of Jewish immigration at the turn of the century further boosted the community. Between 1920 and 1960 there were up to 300 Jewish families in Saint John. Today, the

Statues by Sussex sculptor John Hooper, at the Saint John post office

synagogue is in the former Calvinist church, and photos and displays at the Jewish Museum celebrate the city's Jewish heritage.

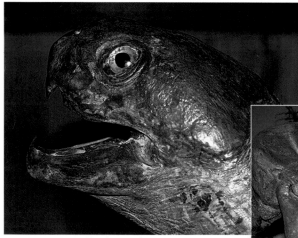

Natural history exhibits at New Brunswick Museum

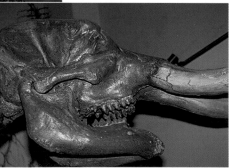

The city prospered from lumbering and shipbuilding. Today, the historic brick warehouses, Boston-style townhouses, impressive homes of merchants, politicians and brewers, the former stock exchange, the first chartered bank, the Bank of New Brunswick with its massive fluted columns and the signs of the Jardine Shipping Line are reminders of the city's rich commercial heritage. The Seamen's Mission on Prince William Street and "The Three Sisters," a red and white street lamp that has helped guide ships into the harbour since 1848, show another side of the city's seafaring heritage. It is no wonder that the Old City Market resembles the inverted hull of a boat, an appropriate symbol in a city made rich by shipbuilding. The design was the result of a competition among local architects. Since 1877, the market has been both a meeting place and a farmers' market for residents and visitors, offering a wide variety of foodstuffs — lobsters and dulse, meat and cheese, apples and baked muffins. For visitors who want to discover historic urban Saint John, brochures of three walking tours — "Prince William Walk," "Loyalist Walk" and "Victorian Walk" — are available at tourist centres free of charge.

Like other Maritime centres, Saint John shared in the wartime booms of 1914 and 1939. A local entrepreneur,

Saint John's Reversing Falls

Nestled in the restored Market Square amongst shops, pubs, cafés, wooden sculptures, fountains and the Saint John Free Public Library, the New Brunswick Museum boasts amazing displays that bring the province's natural history alive. It is Canada's oldest museum, featuring a geological trail, the Hall of Great Whales and fine and decorative art galleries. The preserved fossil bones of a huge American Mastodon, trapped in mud and found in a New Brunswick lake in 1936, are displayed in skeleton form on the second floor. This fossil is one of the most complete mastodons found in the Maritimes. The skeletons of a rare northern right whale, a sperm whale, and a minke whale are impressive displays of sea mammals found in the Bay of Fundy in summer months.

Reversing Falls is a famous natural attraction in Saint John. An information centre complete with video presentations and a viewing platform is located on a steep cliff overlooking the St. John River near its mouth. When the tide is going out, the river empties into the Bay of Fundy. It does so quite vigorously; there are pools and eddies, and it is not safe for boats to run the rapids. After the tide turns and the water in the bay rises, the pressure of the river water flowing down and the water of the bay pushing up is equal. This is low slack tide and it is safe for boats to pass through — but only for 20 minutes. After that, the water of the bay rises so intensely that it actually pushes the water upriver. For about six hours, water flows upstream. At high slack tide, boats can briefly pass through the narrows until the tide joins the river current, creating turbulent rapids at the river's mouth.

K.C. Irving, moved to Saint John to establish a car dealership and went on to build an industrial empire that transformed the province's economy. By 1949, he owned the region's largest bus carrier, all the English-language daily newspapers in Saint John and Moncton, several sawmills, a paper mill, vast forest holdings, Saint John Dry Dock and an ever expanding string of service stations, selling products from the Irving refinery at Saint John. By the 1990s, the second and third generations of Irvings were carrying on the family tradition. The Irvings' tribute to the people of Saint John is the Irving Nature Park on the Taylor Peninsula, an eco-tourism site with nature trails.

Market Square, Saint John

Fundy National Park

Fundy National Park, for short "Fundy," covers a natural region of 206 sq km (80 sq mi), laid out in a rectangle roughly 13 km by 16 km (8 mi by 10 mi). Here the Acadian Forest of the Caledonia Highlands meets the great tides of the Bay of Fundy. The highway through the park is steeper than most roads in southern New Brunswick. A lookout just before the road tumbles down to sea level provides a memorable view of the blue waters far below. The park's landmark is the covered bridge at Point Wolfe, which was recently replaced after it was accidentally destroyed by a work crew while blasting.

Fundy boasts a variety of ecosystems: from the windswept cliffs along the bay to large stands of beautiful hardwoods; from boggy swamps to deep gorges with roaring waterfalls. Founded in 1948 to protect the region's natural and cultural heritage, the park manages wildlife and ecological programs, and the park rangers offer interpretive walks and evening events.

Irish, Scottish and English settlers in the early 1800s once made their homes along the bay to take advantage of the fertile lands, but those settling in the cold highlands along Shepody Road, which now forms the northern border of the park, were faced with misery and hardship, because the soil was rocky and the growing season too short. They soon had to abandon their farms and move to the milder area near the coast. There, however, the good lots had often been already claimed. Many families settled in Herring Cove and in what is now the village of Alma, just outside Fundy National Park. The best farmland in Fundy was found in the high-priced lots along the coast where rivers and brooks entered the Bay of Fundy. John Matthew was one of the first to arrive and he obtained a land grant at Herring Cove. His farm and his son's neighbouring farm flourished. Today, remains of the former Matthew homestead with rock foundations can be found by hiking down to Matthews Head.

Between Matthews Head and Alma near today's swimming pool, Otis Cannon built and operated a small sawmill and a tide-powered fishing weir. At the western park boundary, the Point Wolfe River and the Goose River were once the major sites of water-powered lumber mills. By 1826, the mill town of Point Wolfe was founded, wharves were constructed in the estuary and the virgin forest was harvested to build the city of Saint John and the fortune of John Ward, a former New York Loyalist. Today, the Goose River Trail passes by old fields now overrun with raspberry bushes and an overgrown school yard — reminders of the settlement at Goose River. Further logging activity was carried out upriver. Today, part of the East Branch Loop uses a former hauling road which leads

Matthews Head, Fundy National Park

to the remains of an old logging dam at the East Branch River. Tall red spruce trees and stately white pines were hauled to the East Branch and floated down to the mill at Pointe Wolfe.

The people who settled this region are long gone and their homesteads and fields have been reclaimed by forests as wilderness is allowed to return. Despite the aggressive harvesting of red spruce up until the park's foundation, remnants of older red spruce still stand. They are characteristic of the Maritimes' Acadian Forest. Old growth can still be seen along the Coastal Trail starting at Pointe Wolfe. A climb leads to the big red spruce trees distinguished by their rust-coloured twigs. Some virgin red spruce, up to 350

years old, may still exist in steep stream valleys that are difficult to harvest.

Under the conifers, there are ferns, mosses and other shade-tolerant plants that sprout from the acid soil, including bunchberries, wood sorrel, Clintonia lily, wild sarsaparilla, wild lily-of-the-valley, twinflower and the white Indian Pipe. Yellow birch, maple and beech trees form the beautiful hardwood ridges found in Fundy. Trout lily, red trillium and red elderberry mixed with ferns blanket the forest floor. The Acadian Forest is best represented as a mixed forest. In this largest portion of the park, hardwoods intermingle with softwood trees. Painted and white trillium, pink lady's-slipper orchid, the starflower and many fungi prefer this forest. Nurse logs line the trails: hardwood seedlings sprout in the moist soil provided by fallen, decomposing trees. Some of these new trees will have long exposed roots, well off the ground, a sign that they grew atop a log, which rotted away over time.

In 1982, a successful four-year program was undertaken in Fundy National Park to save peregrine falcons, which were close to extinction in eastern North America. For almost a century, Atlantic salmon were barred from their spawning ground upriver by a dam. In 1982, in a restoration effort by Parks Canada and the federal Department of Fisheries and Oceans, 42,000 fingerlings reared in a fish hatchery were carried to selected pools in the river by helicopter. Today, coyote, deer, moose, black bear, raccoon and beaver live in the park. Encounters with wild animals can be enjoyed and are safe, provided that campers keep a safe distance, keep their campsites clean and don't attempt to feed the animals.

Fundy National Park offers a range of activities, from camping, hiking and mountain biking to boating and bird-watching, tennis and golf, as well as swimming in a heated saltwater pool.

Fundy Coast

The Bay of Fundy is a remarkable marine environment. In addition to whales and other sea mammals, thousands of shorebirds rest here among some unique geological formations enjoying the benefits of the highest tides in the world. The late Melville Bell Grosvenor, former president of *National Geographic* magazine, loved exploring the Fundy coast. Every summer, he spent a couple of weeks hiking and bird watching in what he called "one of the most beautiful places on earth." High praise from a man who knew where to find the secret beautiful spots in the great outdoors. Many tours await adventurous types in the Fundy area. From late spring to late summer, travellers can watch finback whales, humpbacks, minkes, and right whales up close. Not far from the Fundy

Hopewell Rocks

National Park is the picturesque Cape Enrage, a steep rocky cliff, which invites exhilarating activities such as rappelling and sea kayaking, and less strenuous activities, such as searching for fossils on the shore at low tide.

At Mary's Point, during the first half of August, hundreds of thousands of shorebirds rest here on their migratory route. A narrow footpath sloping down past the interpretation centre to the beach offers the best vantage point for observing the birds. Sandpipers and plovers of various subspecies congregate here on the mudflats after the tide goes out. They feed on tiny mud shrimps and worms. In mid-August, well fed and rested, the birds are ready for the four-day flight to their winter habitat in northern South America. Among the birds that roost on the beach is the Semipalmated Plover, a chubby little bird with a single black band across its white breast. Its flying and roosting companions are the fairly large, orange-legged Ruddy Turnstone and the Semipalmated Sandpiper.

One minute the flock roosts and the next, amidst a sudden wave of flashing dark and silvery light, a dense clump of birds arcs swiftly into the air along the shore, gracefully shifting this way and that. Then they settle down on the beach and repeat their spectacular performance a little while later. A truly amazing natural show. Another important migratory site is located across Shepody Bay at Dorchester Cape.

Birdwatching at Mary's Point

seaweed with small oval bladders at its tips. There is certainly nothing quite like the Bay of Fundy anywhere else in the marine world.

New Brunswick's first-rate natural wonder along the Fundy Coastal Drive is Hopewell Rocks, the only place in the world where tides as high as a four-storey house can be seen. Twice a day, one hundred billion tonnes of saltwater makes its way in and out of the Bay of Fundy. The rise and fall of the ocean is the result of the gravitational forces of the sun and moon. The tidal effects are the same all over the world, but here they are more visible due to the length and shape of the bay, which acts as a funnel, pushing the water inward. As there is no exit, the water level rises dramatically. The average change in water level at Hopewell Rocks is 10.7 m (35 ft). The largest change ever measured there was 14.8 m (48.6 ft).

At high tide, the Rocks aren't very impressive, but when the tide falls, the fascination of the place immediately becomes apparent. Then you can walk down the three flights of iron stairs and stroll on the ocean floor, around the base of the "Flower Pot" islands, now towering towards the sky. Some of the ocean floor is soft, wet sand, some is mud with tidal pools and some is rock. The reef is a surprisingly solid conglomerate rock. The exposed surface is blanketed with barnacles, small cone-shaped shells. Next to them grows rockweed, a curious

Rapelling at Cape Enrage

Eastern Fundy Coast

A short distance from Hopewell Rocks on Route 114 is the Albert County Museum complex, including the courthouse, jail and agricultural building. The stately courthouse was built in 1904 to replace the original 1846 building, which burned down in 1902. The prominent style is Classic Revival, and its most unusual feature is the ceiling decoration of pressed tin. The courtroom contains a prisoner's dock, witness stand, raised seating area and a public gallery.

Across from the courthouse is the museum, which houses three cells of the former jail with massive 26-inch walls, and 3-inch iron bars on the windows. Particularly chilling is the dungeon — a cell used for solitary confinement with a big iron ring in the centre to which unruly prisoners in leg irons were anchored. The wooden door has an axe mark: it played a part in one of the most famous murder trials in the country, the so-called "Rectory Murder." In December 1906, the housekeeper

Railroad museum, Hillsborough

of the parish priest was brutally murdered in the course of an attempted robbery, while the priest was out of town. Evidence seemed to point to Tom Collins, a young man who had come from Ireland only months before. He had worked as handyman around the rectory near Riverside-Albert. After the murder, Tom Collins vanished but was quickly captured and tried in the county courthouse next door. At his third trial he was sentenced to death and he was hanged in 1907. He never confessed to the crime. The fascinating story is retold by Ken Saunders in *The Rectory Murder*.

The adjacent large barn contains a complete pioneer kitchen and a lot of farm equipment, including a stump harrow, treadmill and butter churns. One of the more unusual items is a dog treadmill.

In the heart of Albert County lies Hillsborough, a village known for its historical trains and as the birthplace of William Henry Steeves, one of the Fathers of Confederation. New Brunswick's only surviving steam engine and coach car, operated by the Salem and Hillsborough Railroad Inc., is permanently stationed at Hillsborough. An excursion on board

Steeves House, Hillsborough

the train leads through beautiful countryside, past fields, forests and marshes. On its journey, with some effort and a lot of steam, the train's engine, dating back to 1899, huffs and puffs on the climb out of the valley and across a trestle bridge, while the passengers relax in a 1914 railroad car trimmed with luxurious wood panelling. Back at the station, a small railroad museum offers a captivating display of railroad memorabilia and railway equipment.

On Mill Street stands the imposing white panelled Georgian-style Steeves House. William Henry Steeves, who was the owner of a shipbuilding company and grocery store, and who later became one of the Fathers of Confederation, was born in this house in 1814. His parents, Heinrich and Rachel Stief, were immigrants from Germany, who later

Albert County Museum (left and right)

anglicized their name to Steeves. The original house was built in 1812 and had only two rooms. When the house was sold by William Henry Steeves, it passed through the hands of several managers of the nearby gypsum mill, who enlarged the building. The living room is furnished with both a desk fashioned from a pump organ and an unaltered Estey Pump Organ from the Hillsborough Baptist Church with the likeness of the organ builder and his wife carved into the wood.

The staircase has an unusual feature: a number of steps have prisms in them. Whenever the lady of the house required maid service, she would place a lantern beneath the stairs. The light shone through the prism, signaling the maid, who lived upstairs.

The upstairs exhibits include a rope bed in the children's room. The rope had to be made taut each night, otherwise the bed would sag, thus giving rise to the saying, "good night, sleep tight." The Grapevine Quilt in the bedroom, made by Maria Steeves in 1834, received a first prize in New York. Unfortunately, a jar of jam was wrapped inside it, and broke on the way back to New Brunswick. The jam stains remain to this day. Still, with its vibrant colours, the Grapevine Quilt is recorded as one of the finest textiles in Canada.

Southeastern New Brunswick

Set amid the sprawling Tantramar Marsh and the award-winning Waterfowl Park, the town of Sackville delights nature lovers. In 1988, after a long effort and with a lot of cooperation, the pretty university town created a waterfowl park in the heart of town. The CN Railway gave the right-of-way, Mount Allison University and the town of Sackville provided some of the land, and Ducks Unlimited installed the dykes and water control structure. At one time,

Sackville Waterfowl Park

the whole area was a salt marsh, but the first dykes were built in the 1600s when Acadian settlers farmed here.

The Waterfowl Park is part of the larger Tantramar Marsh, a name that stems from the French word *tintamarre*, for the "noise" or "racket" made by birds. In the summer of 2001, the Waterfowl Park was extended to the northern section of the greater Tantramar Marsh, providing a habitat for about 130 species. According to naturalist Dr. Paul Bragdon, about two dozen birds actually breed here. Mallards, Blue-winged teals and other species, as well as muskrats can be viewed from the boardwalks that zigzag through the park or from the wooden observation tower. Along this nature walk, plaques give explanations about different species and their behaviour: dabblers and skimmers simply reach below the water to feed, but divers, such as Grebes, dive down for minnows and other small fish.

Sackville is also a town for fine and performing arts, reflecting the university's specialities. Live Bait Theatre, summer concerts in the park, along with art galleries and craft shops give this town a special flare. Another Sackville attraction is the Harness Shop, a genuine workshop and the only one of its kind still operating in North America. The front part of the house was built in 1845, but a fire in 1991 caused extensive damage on the upper floor. It opened in 1919 and has been going strong ever since. Currently, it has three employees — they are highly trained to make horse harnesses and collars, as well as leather school bags, handbags and belts, and repair work. They use traditional equipment, such as a sewing machine that is about 70 years old. This is also the only place in North America that still makes straw-filled collars!

Not far from Sackville, on the provincial border with Nova Scotia, is the site of a fortress where two nations once fought for dominance in North America. Perched on a hill, Fort Beauséjour overlooks the vast marshlands created by dykes built by the Acadians 400 years ago. In the early

Mount Allison University Campus

structure Fort Cumberland. This imperial conflict brought about the expulsion of over 5,000 Acadians.

Fort Cumberland was prominent again during the American War of Independence when a small group of revolutionaries attacked it. The same summer, 200 Yorkshire settlers arrived to restore the damaged fort and defend the British colony against American forces. Today, names on mailboxes such as Yeoman, Black, Truman, Dixon and Keillor are reminders of these Yorkshire descendants.

In 1926, the fortress was declared a national historic site, bearing its former French name Fort Beauséjour. The museum displays seven paintings by Lewis Parker illustrating scenes of the fort from 1754 to 1778. A short slide show depicts the circumstances of the British attack from a French perspective. The museum also holds what is reputed to be the smallest book in the world, a miniature volume less than an inch square containing 100 pages of extremely thin paper. It is a Schloss's *English Bijou Almanac*. Other artifacts relate to the Mi'kmaq Indians, the railroads and dyke-building. Today, visitors can walk on the fort's star-shaped walls and look out across the marshes and dykes or explore the sombre stone casements and barracks.

1750s, England and France had achieved an uneasy peace in Europe, but this meant precious little in the far away colonies. England began building forts throughout Nova Scotia in order to protect its settlements. One was Fort Lawrence. The French quickly responded by building a neighbouring fort — Fort Beauséjour.

The structure underwent several construction stages. In 1751, it was only a palisade, which was strengthened in 1752 when hostilities seemed imminent. In 1754, a secretary at Fort Beauséjour informed the British about French military plans. The British decided to attack first. When the French learned about the impending attack, they sent an appeal for help to Fortress Louisbourg at the Northern tip of Nova Scotia. At the same time, they prepared for the attack by burning all wooden structures that might ignite under cannon fire. The British launched an attack from 38 boats that sailed up Chignecto Bay, carrying 2,000 militia, along with cannons and supplies. In early June, the British began their siege by digging trenches and bringing cannons into position. News arrived from Fortress Louisbourg that no reinforcements would be sent, and when a direct hit destroyed one of Fort Beauséjour's casements, the French surrendered. The victorious British forces renamed the

Fort Beauséjour

Moncton

Thomas Williams House, Moncton

world where Acadian dining, music and festivals can be sampled, and where the Acadian *joie de vivre* is always in evidence.

The Acadians' ancestors came to this region from western France between 1632 and 1635. They gradually developed self-sufficient agricultural communities along the Bay of Fundy, where fertile marshes and high tides ensured healthy grain surpluses for trade with New England. With the construction of Halifax and other English settlements as an answer to France's strengthened military posts in Nova Scotia, the British considered the Acadian communities a threat to stability. In 1755, they decided to drive the Acadians from their homes. Fourteen thousand Acadians were deported from their lands; they found their way to New England, Quebec, France, Prince Edward Island, the Magdalen Islands and in the course of time to the southern colonies. In 1758, a proclamation issued throughout the British colonies invited settlers to claim the unoccupied Acadian farmlands. When the British government permitted the Acadian exiles to return in 1764, providing they dispersed throughout the area, they found their lands taken and many went further up the coast to the Bay of Chaleur in northern New Brunswick.

Famous for its sandy beaches and some of the warmest salt water north of Virginia, New Brunswick's Acadian Coastal Drive stretches 477 km (300 mi) from Aulac to Campbellton. Four hundred years of Acadian history and eons of natural history have shaped this region into a surprise of nature, culture, cuisine and celebrations. The Acadian Coastal Drive is one of the few places in the

It is somewhat ironic that the predominantly French city of Moncton bears the name of Lt-Col. Robert Monckton,

Free Meeting House, Moncton

who led the British troops that had uprooted Acadians during the Seven Years' War (1756-1763). In 1766, eight families, mostly of German descent, came from Pennsylvania and settled at "The Bend," where a memorial is erected at the landing site. Some of these German pioneer families and permanent settlers were named Trites, Steeves and Lutz — surnames that are frequently found on mailboxes in the Sackville-Moncton area today.

Moncton's oldest surviving building is the Free Meeting House next to the city museum. Its spartan interior consists of grey box pews and a raised pulpit. Built in 1821 and true to its name, it has been used over the years by Baptists, Methodists, Presbyterians, Roman Catholics, Reformed Episcopalians, Free Christian Baptists, Reformed Presbyterians, Seventh Day Adventists, Jews, Pentecostals and the Christian Science Church.

The Moncton Museum features the history of the city from the age of sail to the age of rail, to the present. One particularly noteworthy artifact is a railway wheelbarrow made of butternut wood on the outside with birdseye maple as interior lining. Another exhibit provides historical information on dyke-building, including a display of tools.

In the nineteenth century, Moncton prospered on thriving industries: the cotton mill, Thorne's Sugar Refinery, Givan's Steam Laundry, the J.A. Marven Biscuit Factory and the Intercolonial Railway. Thomas Williams, the treasurer of the railway, his wife and 11 children lived in an 1883 Victorian Gothic-style house on Park Street.

Today, the Thomas Williams House and Tearoom is operated by Heritage Moncton Inc. The home is decorated with period furniture and the front porch tearoom makes this a lovely place to visit. One of the prettiest parts of the house is the upstairs hallway with its hardwood floors and alcove. On the rooftop there is the ragged remains of once-elegant wrought iron cresting. The story goes that while Mr. and Mrs. Williams were away, one of their sons developed a craving for candy. Finding none in the house, he climbed onto the roof, took down some part of the cresting that he could reach and sold it to a junkman to get money to buy treats!

Bore Park in downtown Moncton offers a fine view of the tidal bore, a natural phenomenon of the Petitcodiac River. When the tidewater comes upriver, it creates a turbulent wave that bores its way through the current. Depending on the position of the moon and sun, the wave may be either a small upsurge or a flood wave. This spectacular scene is worth waiting for: it presents the transformation of a mudflat into a river under 7.3 m (24 ft) of water.

Perhaps the most famous attraction near Moncton is the "magic" of Magnetic Hill. Here, a

Downtown Moncton

stretch of dirt road appears to be sloping downwards. Guides direct cars to the "bottom" of the road, from where they roll backwards "up" to where they came from — a fascinating natural phenomenon and illusion.

Southeast Beaches

The Acadian Coastal Drive winds its way up the Acadian Peninsula along the scenic red- and white-sanded coastline of the Northumberland Strait. For centuries, the strait has been a barrier between New Brunswick and Prince Edward Island. Before the ferry and the bridge, people crossed the strait from Cape Traverse to the mainland at Cape Jourimain by small ice-boats in winter. It was hard, dangerous work to paddle the exposed boats in open water, to drag them through floating ice chunks, and haul them like sleds over solid ice. For decades, Cape Tormentine, an outcrop near Cape Jourimain, has been the home of the New Brunswick ferry service to the Island.

Plans for a permanent link were made three times after Confederation — a challenging undertaking due to environmental concerns and the extremely difficult ice and water conditions of the Northumberland Strait. After 10 years of studies and court challenges, public hearings and plebiscites, the mega-bridge was finally built. It opened in May 1997. The aptly named Confederation Bridge, now celebrated as the largest salt-water bridge in the western hemisphere, connects to the Island and the mainland by a two-lane highway 11 m (36 ft) wide. The "fixed link," as it is often called, stretches more than 13 km (8 mi) across the sea. The structure is raised in its middle section, reaching a height of 64 m (210 ft).

Cape Tormentine and the Cape Jourimain Nature Centre at the mainland base of the Confederation Bridge offer the best vantage points for the bridge and the lighthouses on the promontories. Cape Jourimain is located on a major migratory route. A 600-hectare (1,500 acre) wildlife sanctuary with 13 km (8 mi) of trails has been set aside at the Cape Jourimain Nature Centre. For a fee, the centre offers access to the trails, a four-storey tower, and an interactive exhibit hall featuring displays on ecology, history, climate, transportation and 170 species of birds. There is also a restaurant and an information centre.

Up the scenic coast is Cap-Pelé with beautiful beaches and low tide sandbars that keep the water warm in

Confederation Bridge

Kelly's Beach, Kouchibouguac

Salt marsh, Kouchibouguac

summer. The newly erected Aboiteau Beach Complex at Cap-Pelé includes a small vacation village with boardwalks and bright wooden cottages that adorn the shore. Nearby is Shediac, a lively town which caters to many visitors. A huge lobster statue, weighing 90 tonnes, is displayed at the Rotary Park — after all, this is the lobster capital of the world. During the annual Shediac Lobster Festival, parades, races, Acadian music, fireworks and lobster delicacies are on the menu.

Just north of Shediac is Parlee Beach Provincial Park boasting New Brunswick's favourite swimming beach. Visitors may also indulge in windsurfing, beach volleyball, amphitheatre performances, picnicking and camping. Touch football tournaments, the triathlon and the sand-sculpture contest are annual events.

Further up the Acadian coast is the Irving Eco-Centre: La Dune de Bouctouche, a nature sanctuary *par excellence.* The Mi'kmaq called this place "great little harbour," and the Acadians returning from exile in the late eighteenth century settled here. They saw

Cape Jourimain Lighthouse

Bouctouche's natural harbour as a future commercial port in their new Acadia. The sand dune, created within the har-

bour during the last ice age was an important geographical feature to the fishing industry, in that it served as shelter for fishermen and their boats. In recent years, J.D. Irving Ltd. developed this dune as a shelter for wildlife and as an educational centre for the public, especially school children, to learn more about the dune, its ecology, shorebirds, mammals, plants and insects. The 2-km (1.3-mi) boardwalk on the dune and through the salt marsh allows visitors to observe the dune's wildlife without disturbing the delicate surroundings. Adventurous types may want to walk the complete 12-km (7.5-mi) length of the sand dune to the lighthouse, a five- to six-hour return trip.

Established in 1969, the sizable Kouchibouguac National Park has 24,000 hectares (71,000 acres) and is the largest park in the province. The name Kouchibouguac derives from the Mi'kmaq language, meaning "river of the long tides." The park is basically flat land shaped by glaciers. Its major attractions are marine environments — salt marshes, the seashore, sand dunes, bogs and beaches. The water temperature in shallow lagoons may reach 20°C/68°F in July and August. Major activities — other than swimming and beachcombing — are biking, canoeing and some hiking. Bird watching is also excellent along the shore and on the marshes.

Bouctouche

Musicians at Pays de La Sagouine, Bouctouche (top);
Pier to Pays de la Sangouine (below)

Parents sent their girls there at a time when standing in the community and gentle breeding were paramount. Life in the convent was strictly regulated for the 80 girls who lived here under the watchful eyes of Mother Superior: mass, breakfast, classes, lunch, afternoon classes, mass, garden work, then one hour leisure time, and to bed at nine. Most girls who graduated from the convent became teachers.

At the north end of Bouctouche sits the cottage of Antonine Maillet, the writer who created Acadian anti-hero *La Sagouine*. The new theme park at the edge of town, *Pays de la Sagouine*, is based on this fictional washerwoman, and the characters and houses on the site draw from the novel. A wooden tower provides a view of the park, including a natural island and a long, winding boardwalk that leads to it. At the visitor centre, a short bilingual film presents the play's idea and an introduction to the Acadians. At times, Acadian music is performed and a rendition given in French of a monologue from the play. Antonine Maillet wrote in 1984 that her birthplace was "balanced between two extremes: between a billionaire Irving and a Sagouine on her knees before her scrubbing pail; between the adventurers of the seas and the tillers of the earth; between the wealth of its traditions and its progressive ambitions; between its memory of the past and its dreams of the future."

Though he left here in 1925 for Saint John and later Bermuda, the late K.C. Irving's presence is still felt everywhere in Bouctouche: in the Irving Station and convenience store; in Kent Homes Ltd., the prefabricated-home factory; the white oil tanks; the donated carillon at St. John the Baptist Church and the main street that both

Exploring the natural beauty of Kouchibouguac National Park and the sand dune at the Irving Eco-Centre is a must for visitors, but there are also heritage sites to discover in their vicinity. The village of Bouctouche is the birthplace of both the Acadian author Antonine Maillet and the industrialist K.C. Irving.

Until 1964, the French village was also home of the Roman Catholic convent school for girls. The walls of the Kent County Museum and Old Convent recall the days when the Church took a keen interest in both the temporal and spiritual education of its youth — hence the convent.

Rexton's Bonar Law Historic Site

bear his name; and at the 12-km (7.5-mi) sand spit and eco-centre. He started out in town with a small gas pump and a Ford car dealership, and by sheer determination built his own business empire. Although he and his family rose to become among the world's richest with business interests including a shipyard, a refinery, supertankers, pulp and paper mills, tree farms, prefab homes, newspapers, hardware stores, gas stores, restaurants, bus companies, a frozen food business, trucking and so on, the Irvings lived quietly in New Brunswick, largely unknown to the rest of Canada.

Picturesquely located on the bank of the Richibucto River is Rexton's Bonar Law Historic Site, the old boyhood home of Bonar Law, who became Britain's only prime minister born outside the United Kingdom. In 1850, his father, the Reverend James Law, purchased the nine-hectare (22-acre) farm and established a Presbyterian manse. Today, costumed staff carry out daily chores at the provincial site, which consists of the house supplied with late nineteenth-century furniture, barns full of sheep, pigs and turkeys, farming implements, a garden and picnic place. An interesting feature is the "beggar's bench" near the entrance. It opens into a bed — a useful feature for unexpected guests.

Another nostalgic journey, going even further back in time to the 1820s, is provided by the MacDonald Farm Historic Site at the Miramichi Bay in Bartibog. The land is not much different than it was when Alexander MacDonald settled here. He had served as a private soldier with the British Forces in the War of Independence. He

MacDonald Farm Historic Site, Bartibog

became a justice of the peace and was considered well off. The seven-room farmhouse, constructed with stones that came from Scotland as ballast, was home to MacDonald, his wife and their 13 children. Jellies and jams from the olden days, still preserved by a thick layer of wax, line some kitchen shelves. A spice canister with a lock suggests how precious spices were in those days. Upstairs is an amazing seven-foot gun used for waterfowl hunting, requiring a steady hand indeed. The original settlers had to work hard to make productive farm land out of the dense forests. The grounds, the wharf and the spring house, and the view across the bay are choice spots for visitors today. And, of course, old MacDonald's farm has animals — among them horses, goats, pigs, turkeys and the occasional cat — a perfect backdrop for an 1820s family farm.

Shippagan

Aquarium and Marine Centre, Shippagan

A drive through the fishing communities along the north-eastern Acadian coast offers ample proof that fishing remains a powerful economic factor despite the recent collapse of ground fish stocks, especially cod. Hundreds of fishermen who live in coastal towns like Shippagan, Caraquet and Lamèque depend on lobster and snow crabs for a living. The "Acadian lobster" is exported worldwide and, according to local legend, the snow crab harvest, which began in the early 1970s, has created at least 18 millionaires. The town of Shippagan is considered the provincial capital of commercial fisheries. In addition, the best seafood restaurants in all of New Brunswick are found in this area.

Shippagan's leading attraction is the Aquarium and Marine Centre. This complex is devoted to the marine world and to the fishing industry past and present. It is also a centre of marine research in the province. The displayed wheelhouse of a modern, hi-tech fishing vessel is an interesting feature — a far cry from the wheels of olden days. The exhibits indicate the great variety of marine species — 125 of them — that inhabit the Gulf of St. Lawrence waters, including crabs, shrimps and urchins, as well as char, dogfish and red hake. The aquarium is home to a large variety of sea life, from the sturgeon with its spiny back to colourful sea anemones.

In the adjacent auditorium a 20-minute show outlines the development of the fishing industry on New Brunswick's shores: after the French were defeated in 1760, Jersey entrepreneurs gained control over the industry for almost a century, employing mostly Acadian fishermen. They

Contemporary Fishing Boat, Wheelhouse Model

Seal at outdoor aquarium, Shippagan

Also in July, Lamèque hosts the International Baroque Music Festival. For more than 20 years this classical music festival has attracted people from near and far. The concert hall for the festival is Sainte-Cécile Church in the parish of Petite-Rivière-de-l'Île. With its perfect acoustics and its pastel-coloured interior of naïve art, the church is a beautiful setting for the festival. Musicians and music lovers can also experience the tranquility and charm of the twin islands Lamèque and Miscou, featuring swimming beaches and the natural beauty of the Lamèque Eco-Parc. Opened in the summer of 2001, the ecological park in Lamèque features flora and fauna of the Acadian peninsula. On a 0.5-km (0.3-mi) boardwalk over water, the interpretive trail leads through the park to an observation tower. The park also offers a nature interpretation centre and gift shop.

practised the barter system, whereby the Acadians delivered their catch to the company in exchange for goods from the company store. In the nineteenth century, Americans began fishing in the bay, in competition with the Jersey company. The latter finally folded in the twentieth century.

There is also an outdoor aquarium, where seals often stretch lazily in the sun. To see them in action, visit around feeding time at 11 a.m. and 4 p.m. They stay outside even in winter, when they are joined by three of their fellows from the Huntsman Marine Centre in St. Andrews.

North of Shippagan is Lamèque Island. During the annual Provincial Peat Moss Festival in July, the town of Lamèque honours the pioneers of the peat moss industry. Activities include a tour of an operating site, where visitors are treated to a demonstration of the harvesting, processing and a state-of-the-art robot bagging operation of the peat moss.

Sea anemones

Caraquet

Acadian Festival

T he northern section of the Acadian Coastal Drive skirts around the waters of the Baie de Chaleur with its beaches, farms and fishing communities. This area is fiercely proud of its Acadian heritage: Acadian cuisine, Acadian fine art and music festivals, cultural festivals, the historic Acadian Village and the Acadian flag. The choice of blue, white, red and yellow painted on mailboxes, lobster traps, garden chairs, barns and boats is not surprising, as these are the colours of the Acadian flag, which proudly waves throughout the towns and villages. In 1881, the starred French tricolor was adopted by the Acadians as their national flag. The yellow star was inspired by the papal colours. August 15, the Feast of the Assumption, has been Acadia's National Day since 1881 and every year communities celebrate this anniversary with gusto. It underlines the importance of the Roman Catholic Church as the institution that took an interest in the lives of the Acadian people. The Church established elementary schools and, in 1864, a French-language college in nearby Memramcook.

The town of Caraquet, founded in 1758, hosts special Acadian Day celebrations that mark the end of a week-long

Acadian colours

celebration with church masses, the blessing of the fleet, dances and plays. The most colourful and unusual event of this festival takes place on the Boulevard St. Pierre — Caraquet's main street — where a few blocks are closed off to traffic. Sharp at 6 p.m., the Tintamarre madness begins. Residents dress up and make a great racket using pots and pans, whistles and cowbells, inviting neighbours and visitors to join in. What is a pain to the ears is a feast for the eyes. Colourful costumes enliven the scene, but the red, white, blue and yellow of the Acadian flag dominates, whether it is worn as a dress or painted on a face. By about seven o'clock, the riotous parade is over.

The Acadian Museum in Caraquet promotes the culture, art and history of the area. A mini-gallery

Acadian Museum, Caraquet

exhibits works by artists from the Acadian Peninsula and displays a collection of unusual and unique theme booths. One unusual item, dating back to 1818, is an aspergillum, or holy sprinkler, used to sprinkle holy water in the Catholic Church.

The importance of the Church for Acadians is represented not only by the yellow star in the flag, representing *Stella Maris* (Star of the Sea) and the protection and guidance of the Blessed Virgin Mary, but also by a museum devoted to the Catholic tradition. The impressive Pope's Museum in Grande-Anse, the only one of its kind in North America, relates the story of Christianity from its beginnings to the present. There is a picture gallery featuring all the popes, and a replica of St. Peter's in Rome, which was first exhibited in New York in the early 1900s. An audio-visual presentation recounts papal achievements and the impact Christianity has had on world history. An entire room is dedicated to the memory of

Cormorants on Pokeshaw Island

Monsignor Melanson, the first archbishop of Moncton, who, in 1937, founded the order of the Daughters of the Assumption. He was also an avid collector of holy relics.

Near the Pope's Museum is a very different kind of attraction that is equally unique. Pokeshaw Provincial Park overlooks a tiny island, a so-called flowerpot rock or sea stack that nature created over millennia by eroding soft sandstone until it became separated from the mainland. Today, thousands of cormorants nest on Pokeshaw Island. It is quite a sight: the few remaining tree stumps and the rock itself are white from bird excrement and fish left-overs. Although the island looks barren, its vibrant bird colony offers an ever-changing vista.

Another nature sanctuary is Daly Point Reserve off Carron Drive in East Bathurst. The 33 hectares (100 acres) of salt marsh, coastline, fields and mixed forests are preserved and administered by Brunswick Mining and Smelting Corp. Ltd. and the New Brunswick Department of Natural Resources and Energy. A maze of beautiful trails skirt the area to an observation tower at Daly Point, overlooking the bay and the view towards Bathurst. Special attractions include Canada Geese that arrive here on their migratory route in the fall and the rare Maritime Ringlet butterfly.

Village Historique Acadien

Tinsmith at Village Historique Acadien

Ten kilometres (6.2 mi) west of Caraquet is one of the finest and most appealing of New Brunswick's heritage sites — the Village Historique Acadien. Maurice Basque, Director of Acadian Studies at the University of Moncton, describes it as "the best place to leap into the past and feel the atmosphere" and learn about daily life in Acadia in the nineteenth century. This award-winning living museum tells the story of the ingenuity and tenacity of the ancestors of the Acadian people after their expulsion in 1755.

Visiting the village will take the better part of a day. This site is more than just a walking tour of various houses — it

Printer at the village

also offers visitors an opportunity to see many old crafts being practised throughout the village and to taste Acadian home-made meals. There are women dyeing and spinning wool, weaving woollen goods and baking bread. The blacksmith shapes square-headed nails on his anvil, while one carpenter makes brooms and another shaves shingles.

The oldest house of about 50 original buildings in the village is the Martin House. Built in 1783, this humble trapper's cabin with a dirt floor once was home to seven people. Some houses have been transported to the site over long distances. The Mazerolle Farm House, built in 1842, was brought here from Mazerolle Settlement, a former French community near Fredericton. Outside the house, the smell of fresh baking lingers as a costumed guide takes loaves out of a traditional outdoor oven.

Riordon Gristmill

Thomas House and outbuildings

strands back, ties them together and — *voîlà*, a new broom! On the other side of the walkway another carpenter shows how shingles used to be made. Further on are the print shop and a small restaurant called La table des ancêtres (the Ancestors' Table), a great place to relax in a rustic atmosphere and enjoy Acadian food.

The blacksmith shop dates back to circa 1866. The blacksmith is usually busy making small implements or square-headed nails for horseshoes. He shapes the red-hot metal, dips it deep into a pail of water, and then offers the cooled product to visitors as souvenirs. At the far end of the village is the mill, also a pre-1900 vintage, which operates several times a day. From the back of the mill is a fine

At the Doucet Farm, a guide demonstrates the art of hand-dyeing wool. She uses all natural colours ranging from red to blue in a variety of earthen tones. Most of the colours are obtained by boiling roots or flowers like goldenrod, which produces a rich yellow. The guide uses one pound of flowers for every pound of dry wool she wants to dye. The blue was traditionally made by dissolving indigo in the urine of a 12- or 13-year-old boy!

The general store has beautiful glass panels imported from Belgium. There is also a tavern, and next to it the carpenter's shop, where broom making is the carpenter's specialty. He starts with the trunk of a young yellow birch, carefully shaving back thin strips of wood without cutting them off. He then folds all the

Baking bread in the outdoor oven

Day with music, dancing and a re-enactment of the Acadian Convention of 1884, at which the three main Acadian symbols were officially chosen — flag, anthem and national holiday. The re-enactments honour secular leaders, such as Pierre-Amand Landry and Pascal Poirier, who helped define Acadian goals and identify these Acadian symbols. The celebrations also honour the priest of Saint-Louis-de-Kent, Father Marcel-François Richard, who proposed the star spangled tricolor flag to the convention in the first place. Richard earned the title "Father of Acadia" for his role in establishing French education and religious institutions throughout eastern New Brunswick. The determination of Acadian priests to promote rural Acadian life, coupled with a naturally increasing birthrate, saw the Acadian population rise from 17 to 28 percent of New Brunswick's population between 1881 and 1911. This boom coincided with a resurgence of group consciousness of the Acadian identity, a cultural revival known as the Acadian Renaissance. The year 2004 marks the 400th anniversary of the arrival by Samuel de Champlain and Pierre Gua de Monts in North America. The village will commemorate and celebrate this significant event with true Acadian *joie de vivre* — no doubt!

Shaving shingles

view of the one-room schoolhouse, the chapel and the mid-nineteenth-century Babineau farm. Past these buildings are the cobbler's shop and the post house, from which a horse-drawn cart offers a ride around the village and back to the entrance.

The village has recently expanded, signifying life in the industrial era — 1890 to 1939. It now includes a shingle mill, a cooper's shop, a tinsmith's shop, a new farm complex, a covered bridge, the lobster hatchery and the Château Albert Hotel, a historical inn offering accommodation for visitors.

Every summer, on August 15, the Village Historique Acadien celebrates Acadian National

Chiasson farm

Doaktown

Canoeing on the Miramichi River

From the capital city of Fredericton to the city of Miramichi, the Miramichi River Route is a 182-km (114-mi) drive through breathtaking salmon-fishing territory. The drive first follows the Nashwaak River and then continues along the mighty Miramichi River. For over 3,000 years, the Atlantic salmon has been harvested in the Miramichi by the Mi'kmaq of Metepenagiag or Red Bank First Nation, New Brunswick's oldest village, which today pays tribute to Mi'kmaq ancestors in a heritage exhibit. The great stands of pine forests at the river's edge attracted British, Irish and Scots to the area as entrepreneurs and lumbermen in the early nineteenth century. The river drives of logs to the mills during the spring freshets are no more, but wood harvesting and pulp and sawmill operations are still economically important for the region.

The area's excellent angling was kept a secret by Miramichi residents, but by the 1920s, after the pulp mill industry was firmly established, the locals found a lucrative

Trophy Salmon, Atlantic Salmon Museum, Doaktown

sideline — guiding sportfishermen eager to experience the thrill of reeling in a 9–13 kg (20–30 lb) Atlantic salmon, one of the best fighting fish anywhere. Up along the several branches of the Miramichi, the rich and often famous made their annual pilgrimages to "the camp" — well-appointed fishing lodges located near salmon pools. Over the years, small towns like Blackville and Doaktown developed facilities to serve the needs of sport fishermen. With declining fish numbers, strict fishing quotas were imposed to save the salmon. A hook-and-release-policy was imposed and efforts were undertaken that banned commercial salmon fishing in New Brunswick.

The Atlantic Salmon Museum in Doaktown pays tribute to the King of Game Fish as a source of food and trade in past and present. Equally important is the museum's message that this prized fish is a part of the natural food chain, and that its habitat must be protected for its survival. The message is delivered subtly, to the sounds of splashing water and the clicking of a fishing reel. Unlike Pacific salmon, which spawn once and then die, Atlantic salmon often spawn two or three times. While in the river to spawn, salmon eat nothing. The female digs the nest or redd in gravel, and deposits her eggs there — about 800 eggs per pound of her body weight. They are then fertilized by the milt from the male salmon. The aquarium allows a close-up view of Atlantic salmon and other fish species.

Downstairs are displays of an unbelievable array of

Doak House

tackle. Other displays show poaching gear, including illegal spears, drift netting gear, jig hooks and even dynamite. On the entrance level, in the River Room, is a trophy salmon of more than 30 kg (70 lb) caught on a fly in 1990 in the Restigouche River. The view from the River Room across the Miramichi is very scenic. Visitors can also walk the lush grounds and tour the smokehouse, ice and snow house and a guide's camp.

Across the street from the Atlantic Salmon Museum is the Doak Historical Site, a living museum commemorating the Squire Doak, one of the leading entrepreneurs of the region in the 1800s. At the entrance, a guide in period costume takes visitors across the fields to the Doak House, constructed in 1822. Robert Doak's career reads like this: 1822, overseer of the poor; 1823, supervisor in charge of highways; 1825, justice of the peace; 1826, school trustee; 1829, acting coroner. The Doak family came to New Brunswick from Scotland and were on their way to Kentucky. During a storm, they sought shelter in the harbour of Newcastle (now Miramichi) and soon changed their plans and settled in New Brunswick.

It is noteworthy that the furniture in the Doak House is original and not collected from various buildings as at other heritage sites in New Brunswick. There is a kitchen table, whose legs are stained with pig's blood, deer antlers for a coat hanger and a day bed that can also be used to store items. The living room features a piano organ and a gramophone, items that indicate the wealth of the inhabitants. The adjacent room and the sewing room with its solid wood window shutters were Mrs. Doak's domain. She feared Indian attacks, and wanted the shutters for protection. Upstairs is the boys' room and a room for a live-in minister! The latter room has painted floors, another sign of wealth, and a bed painted green and pink. The barn not far from the house becomes a lively place during the summer, when some animals, which spend the winter on a nearby farm, are "on loan" to the site.

Miramichi

The city of Miramichi is picturesquely located at the mouth of the Miramichi Bay, where the mighty Miramichi River meets the salty waters of the Northumberland Strait. The communities of Newcastle, Douglastown and Chatham, recently brought together in one municipal unit of Miramichi City, are spread out on both sides of the river. Walking trails and the French Fort Cove Park invite the public to enjoy the waterfront by foot, canoe or kayak. The newly erected Ritchie

Irish Festival, Chatham

Wharf Park is a nautical theme park with docking facilities, craft shops, art gallery, playground and picnic area, outdoor theatre and restaurants. A taste of the river's cuisine is a must, when in town. Local specialties are grilled salmon, pheasant stew and fiddleheads picked from the river banks. The Angler's Reel on the banks of the Miramichi in Chatham claims to prepare fresh Atlantic salmon 25 different ways.

Miramichi's most famous son is Max Aitken, who became a newspaper baron in London, a politician and a benefactor. He was made a Lord, and took the title "Beaverbrook" from a Miramichi hamlet he knew as a child. His boyhood home in Newcastle, the old Presbyterian manse, is not far from the town square, where a bust stands in his memory. In the 1940s, Lord Beaverbrook became intensely interested in his roots and, though he remained an influential figure in London's political and financial world for the rest of his life, he made long summer visits to his beloved Miramichi. He asked the local librarian, Louise Manny, one of his childhood school friends, to try to collect some of the old lumbermen's songs he had heard as a boy. Mrs. Manny asked the public for help, and the public

Ritchie's Wharf, Miramichi

made by the early settlers and their descendants. The Irish began coming to the Maritimes in large numbers in 1847 in search of a better life. The potato famine in Ireland was at its worst in 1848 and 1849, and without sufficient aid from the mainland, the Irish had little choice but to flee in ever greater numbers. At least one million had left Ireland by 1851.

The annual walking parade in Miramichi sets the tone for the Irish Festival, with players of Celtic pipes and drums, Irish dancers and hundreds of descendants from the early Irish settlers bearing the names Kelly, Fitzpatrick, O'Toole and Ronan. The parade travels from James M. Hill Memorial High School to Lord Beaverbrook Arena, which is fittingly decorated in Protestant orange and Catholic green, with a neutral white separating the two. Inside, along the walls, vending booths carry Irish music, Irish jewellery and genealogical information on Irish names. For three days, the festival offers an ambitious program of singers, dancers, fiddlers, pipers and drummers. The music ranges from toe-tappin' tunes like "Whiskey in the Jar," ballads such as "Sam Hall" and "Black Velvet Band" to rebel songs like "The Rising of the Moon." Irish children perform traditional figure dancing, reels and slip jig dancing and the Celtic Riverdance. Tin whistle and Irish dancing workshops, book launchings and lectures round off the program. The Irish Festival truly is a celebration of Canada's culture and heritage through song, dance and cultural workshops.

responded with great enthusiasm. She recorded the traditional woodmen's and farmers' songs and presented her growing collection in a Sunday radio show.

In 1958, Louise Manny organized the first Miramichi Folksong Festival, where for three nights scores of the people she had recorded performed on stage at Newcastle's townhall. The singing and these annual festivals have never stopped. The five-day summer event, now organized by Susan Butler, offers a variety of styles, from fiddle tunes such as "Don Messer's Break Down" and "Turkey in the Straw" to Irish, Scottish and modern dances, from medleys of war songs to the thoughtful "Streets of London" and Irish drinking songs. The traditional and contemporary songs of the Miramichi River are still an important component of this famous Folksong Festival. Generally, there are noon luncheon shows at a local hotel, an open air concert at Ritchie Wharf and nightly shows at the Beaverbrook Kin Centre. The festival has seen international performers such as Aubrey Hanson, Jim Morrison, Vivian and Ivan Hicks, Gordon Stobbe and the late couple Eleanor and Graham Townsend, North America's only championship fiddle team.

Miramichi is also home to Canada's first and largest Irish Festival. The Irish Festival in Chatham was an answer to the popular Folksong Festival of the longtime rival, Newcastle. The Irish Festival celebrates the contribution

Lord Beaverbrook's boyhood home

Appalachian Region

Mount Sagamook

The Appalachian Range Route is a 224-km (140-mi) drive from Perth-Andover to Campbellton through North America's oldest mountains, the Appalachians. The route first follows the Tobique River to Plaster Rock, the southern gateway to Mount Carleton Provincial Park, featuring the highest summit in the Maritimes. The route then leads through Saint-Quentin, the western gateway to the provincial park, and a lively French community. The drive winds through the Restigouche Uplands to Kedgwick and from there to Campbellton at the Bay of Chaleur. The rivers and lakes in the Uplands were used as canoe routes by early inhabitants.

The logging industry also used the waterways to float timber to nearby sawmills. Today, the Upper Restigouche River, now a Canadian Heritage River, offers numerous opportunities for recreation. Nestled among the tree-clad hills of the Appalachian region, the Kedgwick Forestry Museum depicts life in a New Brunswick logging camp in the 1930s. The entire Saint-Quentin/Kedgwick area boasts a flourishing maple sugar industry and enjoys a reputation as the Maple Syrup Capital of New Brunswick. At Campbellton's doorstep rises Sugarloaf Mountain, a pocket-sized version of its famous namesake in Rio de Janeiro.

Mount Carleton Provincial Park

Mount Carleton Provincial Park was created in 1969 as a step to preserve wilderness in New Brunswick. It is by far the largest provincial park in the province and boasts Mount Carleton, the highest elevation in the Maritimes, standing 820 m (2,693 ft) tall. Since altitude affects climate, lower temperatures near the peaks are to be expected at any time of the year, along with snow from mid-October to mid-May. Moose, black bears, and deer all live here, even though hunting pressure outside the park has been severe for many years. In the early 1900s, when big game and salmon were abun-

Fire tower on top of Mount Carleton

dant, the area attracted hunters and fishermen from outside the province, particularly from Connecticut. They set up fishing and game camps along the Nictau and Nepisiguit lakes, and sometimes even created trails. The remarkable Mount Sagamook Trail still follows an old path established in the early 1900s by Admiral Spruance, an avid sportsman from Connecticut. A spectacular view from the peak of Mount Sagamook of Nictau Lake and the adjacent mountains makes this strenuous hike worthwhile. The park now has a total of 62 km (39 mi) of hiking and backpacking trails offering scenic views, waterfalls, lakes, summits, rocky ridges, forests and an old fire tower. Other activities are camping, bird-watching, biking, boating and swimming as well as cross-country skiing in winter.

A 40-km (25-mi) drive from Mount Carleton Provincial Park is Saint-Quentin, a service town to the park and also host to the biggest Western Festival in the Maritimes. What started as a forestry workers' festival more than a decade ago developed into a popular full-fledged Western Festival. The highlight of the week-long event is the Super Rodeo, which is held Saturday and Sunday afternoons. The Super Rodeo is presented by cowboys and cowgirls of the professional Quebec Rodeo. The contestants from Quebec, Ontario and New Brunswick are talented bronco, horse and bull riders. They deliver a friendly rodeo competition and show. All 11 different events, including calf roping and goat roping, are crowd pleasers, but when it's time to start the bull riding, the crowd gets really excited. Throughout the competition, the colourful rodeo clowns joke around, but they have another role to play: to prevent any trouble for man or beast. Events are explained in French, but the scores are also given in English, though the action often speaks for itself. After the Super Rodeo, western paraphernalia can be purchased at the small booths on the site, and a hearty supper of charcoal-broiled steaks and chicken is ready for diners.

Super Rodeo at the Western Festival, Saint-Quentin

Highway 17 heads north through the forested hills of the Appalachian Range, where lumbering is a mainstay of the economy. Just past Kedgwick, a wooden lumberman with axe and saw in front of the Kedgwick Forestry Museum signifies the traditional importance of logging in the region. This heritage lumber camp comprises 15 buildings, representing life and work in rural New Brunswick in the 1930s. The Interpretation Centre shows different uses of wood, from hardwood floors and cabinets to maple sugar, shingles and chips. Traditional tools, such as cant hooks, used at the mill to turn wood and pick poles for river drives, are displayed. A short video shows original footage of logging operations 70 years ago, presented by the people who took part in them!

A small cabin next to the centre is a facsimile of the office where weekly cheques were issued to the workers — $4.29 for loggers and $8.55 for teamsters. Nearby is the combined bunkhouse kitchen. The bunkhouse, with an old barrel stove, was the dormitory for up to 70 woodsmen. The kitchen and dining area with the table settings at the other end of the building illustrate the changing times: from aluminum plates used around the turn of the century, to white enamel ware before the Second World War, to plastic plates in the 1950s.

Kedgwick Forestry Museum

scuttled his ship in the shallow waters of the Restigouche Estuary after being trapped here.

In early summer, the town hosts its annual Salmon Festival, celebrating the prized sport fish with delicious treats and tournaments. An impressive 8.5-m (28-ft) sculpture of the Atlantic salmon dominates Salmon Plaza on the waterfront, but it is Campbellton's Sugarloaf Mountain that dominates the scenery. Viewed from Campbellton, it is a two-peaked mountain, just like the famous Sugerloaf in Rio. Viewed from the Acadian Coastal Drive coming from Bathurst, Sugarloaf appears as a one-peaked natural phenomenon. Year-round recreational possibilities such as jogging, hiking and alpine skiing make Sugarloaf Provincial Park a popular destination. The view from the top of Sugarloaf across Campbellton, the Bay of Chaleur and the Gaspé Peninsula is one of the finest in New Brunswick.

Not far from the five-seater outhouse is the teamsters' camp. They had a separate camp for good reasons. First of all, they usually got up at 4 a.m., much earlier than the lumbermen; and, since they worked with horses all day long, they needed their own facilities in which they could repair their harnesses — which they usually did in the evenings. Last, but possibly not least, teamsters tended to smell of horse, something not appreciated by the loggers.

On the premises is also a fire station, a warehouse and a striking red, roofed-in, Bombardier snowmobile that seats about eight loggers. It may be an ugly looking vehicle, but it was a most luxurious one for travel between the camp and the village.

Campbellton is located at the mouth of the powerful Restigouche River. It was off this coast that the last naval battle for the possession of Canada was fought in 1760. The town's museum contains some artifacts from this last naval engagement of the Seven Years' War between a French frigate and a superior British force. The captain

INDEX